TEACHER'S COMMUNICATIONS RESOURCE BOOK

208 Model Letters, Forms, and Checklists for Everyday Use

TEACHER'S COMMUNICATIONS RESOURCE BOOK

208 Model Letters, Forms, and Checklists for Everyday Use

P. Susan Mamchak
and
Steven R. Mamchak

Illustrated by Patricia A. Fox

Prentice-Hall, Inc.
Englewood Cliffs, N.J.

Prentice-Hall International, Inc., *London*
Prentice-Hall of Australia, Pty. Ltd., *Sydney*
Prentice-Hall Canada, Inc., *Toronto*
Prentice-Hall of India Private Ltd., *New Delhi*
Prentice-Hall of Japan, Inc., *Tokyo*
Prentice-Hall of Southeast Asia Pte. Ltd., *Singapore*
Whitehall Books, Ltd., *Wellington, New Zealand*
Editora Prentice-Hall do Brasil Ltda., *Rio de Janeiro*
Prentice-Hall Hispanoamericana, S.A., *Mexico*

Library of Congress Cataloging-in-Publication Data

Mamchak, P. Susan, 1944–
Teacher's communications resource book.

1. Schools—Records and correspondence—Forms.
2. Form letters. 3. School reports. 4. Teachers—
Handbooks, manuals, etc. I. Mamchak, Steven R.
II. Title.
LB2845.7.M36 1985 651.7'52'024372 85-16730

ISBN 0-13-888355-6

Printed in the United States of America

This book is dedicated to those who do—teachers. In particular, it is for you, Kathy Brazas, Evelyn Clayton, Ray Fedak, and Marcia Giger. You are friends in the teacher's room and masters in the classroom. The students who have you are as lucky as we are to be able to call you our friends.

About the Authors

P. SUSAN MAMCHAK is an elementary teacher, conducts workshops in education, is a past member of Toastmistress International, and has held positions throughout education, from substitute teacher to school disciplinarian. In addition to all her regular activities, she also finds time to do extensive public speaking.

STEVEN R. MAMCHAK, currently a high school English teacher, has been involved in public education for over twenty-five years. In that time, he has done public relations work for schools, hosted a weekly radio program on education, and lectured extensively before educators and community members.

How This Book Will Help You

Teachers share a common enemy: lack of time. The *Teacher's Communications Resource Book* will help you to save time. It sometimes seems that there aren't enough hours in the day to teach and help our students, let alone to prepare reports, keep records, compose meaningful communications, write curriculum and lesson plans, and still do all the other paperwork that we're faced with every day.

The *Teacher's Communications Resource Book* provides you with a solution, a way to draw upon the experience of your colleagues in classrooms across the United States, to manage the deluge of paperwork you face.

This *Resource* gives you hundreds of working letters, forms, and samples on a wide variety of topics directly related to teachers and teaching, selected *by* educators *for* educators. Under each topical listing, you'll find examples and models of written communications, forms, reports, and memos that have helped other teachers save time and handle every kind of communication effectively.

These forms and communications are ready to serve you *now*, with only a name change or new date or address. They can be adapted to meet your particular situation, and will help you tame your own "paper tiger," while freeing you to devote your full energies to teaching instead of clerical work.

This *Resource* is made up of three convenient parts. Each part is then divided into sections, offering the particular type of communications-aid you need for students, colleagues, parents, and administrators. For example:

- Do you need to write a letter of recommendation for a student or a colleague? A notice to parents about an upcoming event or activity? A letter of resignation that insures the support of the administration? Then see Part I, "Letters and Notes," for a multitude of samples to meet these particular needs.
- Do you need a permission slip from parents to allow their children to join the safety patrol? A notice to a student about a possible failing grade? A log to keep track of parents not attending conferences? See Part II, "Forms," for ready-to-use examples that range from achievement to workshop.
- Do you need a checklist for kindergarten parents? A sample page for a newsletter? A report to the nurse regarding a student's vision? Then see Part III, "Handouts, Messages, and Informational Communications," for materials that will get the required response.

All of these communications—plus many, many more—are yours to use and reuse. The *Teacher's Communications Resource Book* is not a book that will gather dust on your bookshelf. You will want to keep it on your desk, right beside your class texts and daily plan book, to serve you today and throughout the entire school year.

P. Susan Mamchak
Steven R. Mamchak

Acknowledgments

We gratefully acknowledge the unselfish cooperation and educational expertise of the many educators who helped us in the compiling and writing of this book. Particular thanks are due to Dr. William Gilchrist and Dr. Guy Sconzo of the Middletown Township (New Jersey) Public Schools and Dr. Larry Ashley and Mr. James A. Mullevey of the Tinton Falls (New Jersey) Public Schools for their encouragement and very practical support.

Contents

PART I

Letters and Notes

Section 1

For Administrators

BEHAVIOR

Letter Concerning Behavior

Dear Mr. Teague:

As vice-principal you are in charge of discipline for the ninth grade. It is for this reason that I wish to bring to your attention a matter that holds a potential for disaster if left untreated.

On several occasions I have personally witnessed a ninth-grade boy harass smaller students and demand money from them, threatening to beat them if they refused. I have made a list of the times and dates of all instances, which I shall be glad to share with you.

As you know, this is a matter that must be handled carefully. Obviously, our objective is to protect the "victims" of this "shakedown," but we also wish to do our best to see to it that the perpetrator receives the help and guidance to abandon such an antisocial course.

I await hearing from you soon, and you may rest assured that you will have my full cooperation in ending this problem as soon as possible.

Sincerely,

SPECIAL NOTE: With all letters that you write concerning behavioral problems, it is wise to keep a copy for yourself. Notice, also, that the child's name is never mentioned, that the expressed aim is to help the child, and that supportive evidence for the claim is offered. This could well have relevance should the case ever come to court.

BOARD OF EDUCATION

Letter of Appreciation

Dear Mrs. Latham:

On behalf of the curriculum committee of Northrup Elementary School, I would like to express to you and to the Board of Education our sincere thanks for your recent approval of the reading program we had recommended.

We are deeply aware of the budgetary constraints and pressures placed upon the Board, and we are equally aware that being a Board member is often a frustrating experience. We are extremely grateful, therefore, for your kindness and interest in hearing our proposal and for your subsequent approval of the project.

We have every confidence that the program will be a success and that your confidence in our judgment will be rewarded, just as the children of our township are rewarded by having dedicated people such as yourself serve them on the Board of Education.

Again, you have our thanks for your kindness and quick action.

Yours sincerely,

SPECIAL NOTE: Quite often, sad to say, educators and the Board of Education or School Board do not see eye to eye on certain issues. When they do, and when there is cooperation between the two groups, it is well to acknowledge this.

Petitioning Letter

Dear Mrs. Latham:

Recently, the curriculum committee of Northrup Elementary School placed before you a proposal for a new reading program at the school. After listening to the proposal, the Board voted five to four not to initiate this program in the coming school year.

Naturally, we are disappointed, and while we realize the necessity for budgetary prudence in these difficult economic times, we feel that part of the problem may have been a misunderstanding of exactly what the program entails.

We therefore respectfully request and petition the Board for another hearing on this matter. We base our request on two factors:

1. The vote was extremely close, with a single vote making the difference.
2. Since that meeting, several new facts have come to our attention that modify the budgetary outlay necessary to initiate the program.

We would be happy to meet with the Board in open or closed session, whichever is more convenient. We feel this is such a worthy project that we can do no less than acquaint you with the new facts we have learned.

We look forward to your reply, and we stand ready to meet with you to discuss this most important matter.

Sincerely,

SPECIAL NOTE: Notice that the reasons for the petition are clearly stated and that there is no incentive or even implied criticism of the Board's initial action. One such letter gets more results than any number of letters critical of the Board.

CHILD STUDY TEAM

Letter of Thanks

Dear Dr. Caulfield:

Recently, I referred a student to you on an emergency basis. I felt that my request was urgent, and I was more than gratified with the speed and professionalism with which this referral was handled. Thanks to your quick action not only was a potential trouble spot removed from the classroom, but a child who desperately needed help was able to get the attention his case merited.

Please accept my thanks for your actions on behalf of this student, and please convey my feeling to the other members of your team. As a professional educator, it is comforting to know that there are people such as yourself who are dedicated to providing the help and guidance our students need during difficult times.

If I may ever be of service to you in the future, please do not hesitate to ask.

Sincerely,

SPECIAL NOTE: One obvious advantage of this note is the rapport it will build, which will be helpful in future dealings with the Team.

COMPLAINT

Letter of Complaint

Dear Mr. Benson:

I feel that it is my duty to register a formal protest regarding your cancellation of the scheduled sixth grade dance for May.

While I realize that the recent disciplinary upheaval in the lunchroom was a terrible incident that cannot be tolerated in the school, I would like to respectfully point out that the infractions were committed by a relatively small group with the vast majority of the students taking no part in the throwing of food. Moreover, the students involved were quickly identified by the teachers in charge, and the entire incident was over rather quickly.

I personally feel that it would be unfair to penalize the majority of our students for the irresponsible actions of a few. Certainly, no one would want such potentially disruptive students at the dance, but the majority of our students have proven themselves capable of acting in an acceptable manner.

Therefore, I respectfully request that you reconsider your action in this matter. I have the deepest respect for your judgment, but I honestly feel that this decision may be ill-advised and lead to negative rather than positive repercussions.

If I may be of any service to you, please let me know.

Sincerely,

SPECIAL NOTE: Notice that the complaint to the administrator is kept calm in tone, that opinions are labelled as such, that reasons for the complaint are given, and that the help and respect of the complainant are offered. This letter gets results.

DRUGS

Referral of Suspected Drug Abuser

Dear Mr. Benson:

I wish to report an incident that I observed at 1:35 P.M. on Monday, April 21, 19xx.

At this time, I was serving hall supervision duty on the second floor and was making normal rounds. As I passed the south stairwell, I heard voices, and as part of my duties, I went to investigate them.

I observed two students standing on the landing between floors. The first student handed money to the second student and said, "This is good, huh?" The second student took the money and handed a white envelope to the first and said, "Yeah, this is super pot." At this point they saw me, attempted to run, and were stopped at the first floor by Mr. Meyerson, who was on duty there.

I know both students personally, have the envelope and money in my possession, and am ready to meet with you at your earliest convenience.

Sincerely,

SPECIAL NOTE: Please note that you have accused no one, but merely reported what you saw and heard. Moreover, you have made it clear that you did all this as part of your professional duties. Further actions in this case, it is implied, now lie in the hands of the administrator.

LESSON PLAN

Reply to Administrative Criticism

Dear Mr. DeValle:

When you returned my lesson plans on Tuesday morning of this week, you included a note in which you questioned the wisdom of assigning my students a unit on the book *1984* by George Orwell. Your exact comment was, "Is this a proper book to read? It seems to be rather anti-establishment. I would recommend you get another book."

I thank you for your concern, both for my class and for the students of this school. I must point out, however, that this book is almost universally assessed to be a modern classic: it is antifascist and even anticommunist (Orwell was totally opposed to communism, as his novel *Animal Farm* shows), and has been approved for use in our school and at this grade level by a unanimous vote of the Board of Education.

Since this novel is being used as part of a unit on totalitarian forms of government, I am sure you will agree that it is a necessary part of our curriculum.

I shall be happy to discuss this with you at your convenience. I would like to share in your opinions concerning this matter.

Yours sincerely,

SPECIAL NOTE: Base your reply upon fact, keep calm and polite, and always leave the door open for the future. These are the keys to handling administrative criticism effectively.

RESIGNATION

Letter of Resignation from the School System

Dear Dr. Hartman:

Please be advised that it is my intention to resign my position as a teacher in the Apple Valley School System at the end of the current academic year. This shall supply sufficient notification as required by contract.

In the ten years that I have taught in Apple Valley, I have come to have the highest personal regard and respect for my colleagues and the entire educational staff of this system.

I am leaving in order to take a position that offers twice my present salary. I am certain that you will agree that this is an incentive that I could not ignore, particularly with the economic necessities of raising a growing family.

I shall miss my colleagues and my students as I shall miss working with people of your professional caliber and that of the entire professional staff.

You have my best wishes for continued success.

Sincerely,

SPECIAL NOTE: No matter how you may feel personally, a letter of resignation is no place to air grievances. Too many people who have done this have later been forced to eat their words. Therefore, it is best to keep it short, to the point, and pleasant.

Letter of Resignation from an Extracurricular Activity

Dear Mr. Morton:

As you know, I have served as drama coach of this school for the past six years. I have enjoyed this activity as well as the support and fine words of encouragement and praise of yourself and other members of the faculty and staff during this time.

Recently I have been under doctor's treatment, and I have been advised by my physician to concentrate my efforts on my teaching duties and avoid all other situations of stress. Since you have, on a number of occasions, told me that you appreciate how stressful directing plays and musicals can be, I think you can surmise the rest.

Regretfully, I must resign as drama coach of this school and forfeit the extracurricular contract that goes along with it. I have made this decision now in order to allow sufficient time for you and the Board of Education to find a replacement without any interruption in the drama schedule of this school.

Please accept my resignation from that contract forthwith, but know that I shall lend every ounce of my moral support to this outstanding activity.

Yours sincerely,

SPECIAL NOTE: While you may not legally be required to state a reason for your resignation, it is always good to give one, particularly in a situation such as this where you are resigning from the extracurricular work only. Note, too, that this letter is positive and assumes that the administrator will understand and help out.

RETIREMENT

Acknowledgment of an Administrator's Retirement

Dear Dr. Bailey:

Word reached me recently of your intended retirement next month. May I extend my personal wishes for a peaceful and productive time filled with all the happiness you deserve.

During my years in Rock Township, I have come to know you as a highly professional and competent educator whose foremost concern has always been for the children of this township. I am happy to have served under you.

Again, may your retirement years be filled with joy and the key to a new adventure!

Sincerely,

SPECIAL NOTE: Keep letters to administrators to the point and they will do quite well.

SCHEDULE

Letter of Protest

Dear Mr. DeValle:

Recently I received my teaching schedule for the 19xx–19xx school year. Most of the schedule is logical and even convenient; however, there is a problem with the last period of the day, which I should like to bring to your attention at this time.

My sixth period assignment is in room 93, located on the first floor at the extreme south end of the building. Indeed, it is in this area that all of my other classes of the day are located as well. My seventh period class, however, is located in room 214 which, as you know, is at the extreme north end of the building and on the second floor. It is a distance of one quarter of a mile between these two rooms.

With three minutes' passing time and the necessity of bringing all books and equipment with me each and every day, this room assignment presents a rather large difficulty.

I have checked with Mr. Morrison, who teaches on the second floor for most of the day, and he is willing to trade classrooms with me during seventh period. This would alleviate the problem entirely, and we are both amenable to the change. We did not, however, wish to initiate any change without your approval, for we are mindful of the necessity of keeping an accurate master schedule.

I look forward to hearing from you within the next day or two regarding this matter. Hopefully, this will alleviate a potential trouble spot.

Sincerely,

SPECIAL NOTE: Mistakes happen, but one of the surest ways to make enemies in the administration is to go ahead and do it on your own without keeping them informed. This letter is polite, helpful in tone, places no blame, and offers a sensible solution while acknowledging administrative perogative.

SCHOOL CLUB

Request to Form a School Club

Dear Mr. Benson:

Recently it has come to my attention that a number of our students share a common interest in something that I have pursued since my own childhood—namely, stamp and coin collecting.

I would therefore like to formally request that I be permitted to form a Stamp and Coin Club under school authority. I envision that the club would meet after school every Thursday in my classroom. I assure you that the club would meet all the requirements of the district for a school-chartered activity, that there would be no fees or charges involved, and that the sole criterion for membership would be an interest in stamp and/or coin collecting or a desire to learn about these hobbies.

Since this has been a personal hobby for over 30 years, I feel qualified to act as advisor to this activity. I understand that this advisorship would not be a compensated position as defined by contract.

Stamp and coin collecting is a fascinating and highly educational hobby, and I am certain that the formation of such an activity would benefit the students of our school.

Please let me know your disposition on this matter as soon as possible, as there are a number of students who are anxious to begin.

Thank you for your concern in this matter.

Sincerely,

SPECIAL NOTE: In some school districts, all clubs are chartered by the school, while in others this is not the case. The letter above covers all the necessary ground for those situations where all school activities must be school sponsored.

SUPPLIES

Inquiry Letter Regarding Supply Disposition

Dear Mr. Dawson:

One week ago, on October 10, 19xx, I sent you a request for school supplies, a copy of which is attached. As of this date, I have not received them.

As I indicated on the form, these supplies are vital for a school-approved project that my classes will be starting. We cannot get going, however, until the supplies are on hand for student use.

I am certain there is a good reason for the delay, and I shall be happy to write another request or anything else that may be required in order to expedite matters. I hope you know that you can always count on my cooperation.

I know that this matter will be cleared up soon. Thank you for your cooperation.

Sincerely,

SPECIAL NOTE: You should always keep a copy of all requisitions. Attach a copy of that copy to this letter if it ever needs to be sent. Notice that you have given a reason why the supplies are necessary and even offered your help.

Section 2

For Colleagues

FACULTY AID

Enlisting Faculty Aid

To the Faculty:

On Wednesday, April 19, the drama club will be holding an all-day dress rehearsal for its spring production of MY FAIR LADY, which has its first performance on Thursday evening at 8:00 P.M. As any of you who have ever been involved in dramatics know, the dress rehearsal is an absolutely necessary, highly frustrating, tiring, long and drawn-out affair. Consequently, it cannot be done during a normal activity period, and to hold it at night would present a real hardship to our students and many parents (not to mention one very tired faculty advisor).

A list of the students involved in this dress rehearsal has been given to you, and I am well aware that this process is going to cause some difficulties in the normal school-day routine: many students will be out of classes, and there will be some disruption of your teaching schedules. I also realize that, as in the past, your professionalism and concern for all of our students will make the best of the situation.

One of the greatest comforts I have as the date of the production approaches is the knowledge that YOU are there to help, and that we may count upon your strength to see us through.

I thank you in advance, and want you to know how much I appreciate your support.

Sincerely,

SPECIAL NOTE: Always get personal when you are asking your colleagues for support. Appeal to their professionalism, and you will seldom go wrong. A letter such as this goes a long way toward heading off any resentment that might have been caused had you gone ahead with the activity without first smoothing the way for your colleagues.

PUBLIC RELATIONS

Letter to Faculty

Dear Colleagues:

As you may know, I have been appointed public relations coordinator for our school. What this means is that I'm going to try to help in getting the general public to realize what fine work is going on in this school. I firmly believe that an informed public cannot help but be well-disposed to our school system when they are made aware of the outstanding activities and education that are taking place here every day.

Are you doing something with your class that might be of public interest? Do you sponsor an extracurricular activity that is engaged in a special project? Do you have a student who is "special" in some way? What about you? Will you be receiving a graduate degree? Have you published anything lately? Are you doing some unusual public service?

These are just some ideas, and I am certain that you can think of many more. Don't let potential stories go by unnoticed. If you have any ideas for public relations releases, please see me as soon as possible.

I am certain that our school and your efforts will be shown in the best possible light.

Yours sincerely,

SPECIAL NOTE: If you are ever in the position of handling public relations stories for your school, this type of letter, combined with your personal dynamism, will help bring about the cooperation of the faculty.

QUALITY

Letter on Quality

Dear Mr. Olson:

As the Head Custodian for our school, please accept my thanks for the fine job you and your staff are doing. The excellent quality of your work is reflected throughout the school building, and I notice it every day in my classroom.

Indeed, I cannot praise you and your staff enough. During our recent drama production, the generous support and help of you and your staff was deeply appreciated, and I am certain that we could not have done it without you.

The outstanding quality of your performance indicates that you are people who set high standards for yourselves and take joy in the quality of your accomplishments.

Please convey to your staff my appreciation and accept my personal "thank you" for all you have done.

Sincerely,

SPECIAL NOTE: Any time someone goes beyond what is required and does something of unusual quality, it is only right that he or she be acknowledged.

RECOMMENDATION

Letter for a Colleague

Dear Sir:

Over the past ten years, I have known Mr. Richard Darren as a professional educator and colleague in the Rock Township school system. During this time, we have taught together in the same department at Thornton Jr. High School.

It has been my observation that he is innovative and dynamic in the classroom, infusing his students with tremendous motivation and instilling in them a joy of learning that will serve them throughout life. I have seen him aid without reprimand, correct without disparagement, and teach by example and deed as well as by textbook fact. I know him to be extremely popular with the faculty, and many of his colleagues, myself included, have sought out his counsel and advice. He shares his knowledge graciously, without condescension.

On a social level I know him to be a person of high moral character who has an ability to set everyone at ease. He has a highly developed sense of humor, is bright and inquisitive, and goes out of his way to help without having to be asked.

I would recommend Mr. Darren to you without reservation. Any school with Mr. Darren on the staff would indeed be fortunate.

Sincerely,

SPECIAL NOTE: When writing a recommendation, especially for a colleague, avoid generalities such as, "He's a great guy!" That is not as effective as stating, in a rather detached manner, what you know and have observed as a professional.

RETIREMENT

Acknowledgment of a Colleague's Retirement

Dear Helen:

I have just learned of your plans to retire next month at the end of the current year. May I wish you happiness and joy and a time ahead filled with the richness you deserve.

Over the years it has been my privilege to teach with you. I have witnessed your charm and good humor, your intelligence and expertise, your competence and ability on many occasions. It is my opinion that you represent the best in professional education. Serving with you has been a joy, and I know that I have learned more from you about teaching than I ever did from any textbook.

You shall be sorely missed, but I know that everyone on the faculty and staff knows how well-deserved your retirement is. Listen closely, and you will hear our collective voices saying, "Enjoy your retirement! Well done, Helen, well done!"

Yours sincerely,

SPECIAL NOTE: Anyone who is retiring after a lifetime in the classroom deserves the recognition and thanks of all. It is well, therefore, that we personally acknowledge a colleague who has reached this plateau.

SYMPATHY

Letter for a Colleague

Dear Mr. Higgins:

My heart is with you at this most difficult of times. When I heard of Margaret's passing, a sense of emptiness descended that time has not lessened.

I have had the honor of teaching with your wife and of sharing some moments of conversation with her. A true professional, she was well loved and highly thought of by faculty, administration, and students. She leaves a rich legacy of care and concern for her students that cannot help but inspire the rest of us to try to live up to her standards. She shall be deeply missed.

Please be assured that my prayers and concern are with you. If I may be of service in any way during this sad time, I would consider it a personal honor. Please do not hesitate to call.

With deepest sympathies,

SPECIAL NOTE: Do you know how to compose a perfect sympathy note? Simply say what is in your heart, and you cannot go wrong.

THANKS

Letter to Faculty

Dear Colleagues:

By George, I think you did it! Your cooperation and support made our production of MY FAIR LADY an outstanding success!

From your quiet strength on the day of our stress rehearsal, to the many words of encouragement just at the time we needed them, to your generous donations of time and energy (and sometimes props and costumes!), to your physical support in the audience both alone and with your families, your support has been our salvation and our pride. I know that the students involved feel this way, and you should know that that is exactly my feeling as well.

I am honored to be part of such a professional and generous faculty.

With deep appreciation,

SPECIAL NOTE: If you are going to ask for the cooperation of the entire faculty, then it is only good manners and good sense to publicly thank them when they have given their support. You could post this on the faculty bulletin board, but it would be better to make copies and post one in each teacher's mailbox.

Section 3

For Parents

ACHIEVEMENT

Letter Concerning Student's Achievement

Dear Mr. and Mrs. Payson:

I think we have all become conditioned to expecting bad news whenever we spot certain envelopes in our personal mail. Indeed, a letter from the IRS engenders only slightly more panic than an official envelope from our child's school. That's why I want to make very clear that this letter contains *only good news.*

As you know, I have served as Robert's English teacher for the past year. In that time, I have come to know your son rather well, and I want you to know how highly I think of him. Over the past year, Robert has done an outstanding job in class, maintaining a high academic average and demonstrating a grasp of the subject well beyond his years. His level of achievement has only been matched by his genuinely warm, generous, humorous, and dynamic personality.

In all, Robert's achievement has been outstanding, and it has, indeed, been a pleasure to have had him in class. I can only envy the teacher who gets him next. He is a credit to himself and to you.

I am certain that he will meet continued success throughout his school years to come.

Sincerely,

SPECIAL NOTE: We have found that letters of this type often become treasured keepsakes for families. Too often, our concentration falls on the underachiever or the troublemaker. Writing a letter of this nature will make you feel really good. Try it.

ACTIVITIES

Informational Letter

Dear Parents:

Our Four Rivers Chorus has worked very hard and, in less than four months, has learned and memorized many new songs. Your continued support is very important to the success of our show in June.

In order to accomplish our goal of a really entertaining program—one your child, you, and our school will be proud of—we have established the following dress requirements for the show:

dark blue slacks (not jeans)
short-sleeved, white T-shirt
dark blue socks

If you do not have the above, we are requesting that you borrow them from a friend or relative. It is very important that all chorus members be dressed alike for the performance.

Kindly have your child bring the above items to school by May 21 for approval. If supplying this "costume" is impossible, please let us know as soon as possible so that we may in touch with other sources for you.

Please feel free to contact us if you have any questions.

Sincerely,

SPECIAL NOTE: It has been our experience that parents may grumble, but they truly love to see their children engaged in school activities. An informational letter sets out exact requirements, keeps the parents informed as to what is happening, and even offers aid if the parents cannot meet the requirements. Such communications are appreciated by parents and bring results!

Letter to Arrange a Field Trip

Dear Mr. Greer:

Thank you so much for granting us permission to visit your newspaper offices and printing facilities on Thursday, March 23. Thank you also for arranging two separate tours and tour guides. I know that the children will enjoy this tour, as will I and the other chaperones.

We will be arriving via school bus at approximately 10:00 A.M. Upon arrival, we will inform you of our presence and wait on the bus until a guide arrives. At that time approximately half of our students (22 youngsters) will leave with that tour. The remainder (21 youngsters) will wait on the bus until the second guide arrives and will leave for the tour approximately ten minutes behind the first group. This should keep each tour group small enough so that it will not interfere with the operations of your plant. As each tour is completed, it will return to the bus. I assure you that there will be adequate adult supervision of each group.

I hope that this is acceptable to you, and I am confident that the tours will proceed flawlessly. I shall be calling you the day before our trip just to confirm our schedule.

Thank you again for your cooperation and your selflessness in providing a fine educational experience for our students. I know that they and their parents appreciate all that you are doing for us, as do I.

Sincerely,

SPECIAL NOTE: As we have said before and will say several more times in this book, planning is the key to carrying off any activity without a hitch. Moreover, a letter of this sort assures the people in charge of the facility you are visiting that some serious thought has gone into the visit. Consequently, they are inclined to grant such requests in the future.

APPRECIATION

Letter of Thanks

Dear Mrs. Wells:

How can I tell you how much the class and I appreciated your time and efforts in giving us that marvelous demonstration on proper grooming of pets? I have personally received many comments from the students, several faculty members, and many parents, expressing their appreciation of your efforts. It was an entertaining and highly informative demonstration from which we all benefited.

The class also wanted me to thank "Whistles," your "model," for the demonstration. She is a beautiful animal, and if she is a trifle heavier these days, it is only because she so won the hearts of the class that EVERYONE wanted to share lunch with her!

Thank you for all you did. We deeply appreciate your sharing of your knowledge and expertise.

Yours sincerely,

SPECIAL NOTE: One thing to remember about letters of appreciation is to suit your style to the object of the letter. Note that the style of a letter to an administrator is much more formal than a letter to a parent, which is more formal than a letter to a friend. The secret of any letter of appreciation, however, is simply to be sincere and mean what you say. You cannot go wrong.

ATTENDANCE

Letter Concerning Student's Attendance

Dear Mr. and Mrs. Smith:

I have had your son, Billy, as a member of my English class for almost two months. I really enjoy having him in our class; he is a personable boy with a quick mind and a pleasant personality. I think he has the potential for being an outstanding student.

That is why I must ask for your help with something that concerns Billy's progress. Over the past six months, I have noticed that Billy has been consistently absent from school every Friday. As he may have told you, this has placed an extra burden on your son in terms of having to "make up" the missed classwork, homework, tests, and quizzes, not only in my class, but in other classes as well.

So much depends on a child's day-to-day development that I am becoming concerned about Billy missing so much class time. I am contacting you now because I like Billy and want him to do the best he can.

May I visit you at your home on Thursday evening, November 3, at 7 P.M.? If there is any problem in school that is contributing to Billy's absences, or if I may help in any way, perhaps we could discuss it. If that time is inconvenient, please let me know when we can get together to help Billy.

Thank you for your understanding. I know we can work together for Billy.

Sincerely,

SPECIAL NOTE: Notice how concern for the child is expressed as the foremost priority. This is an excellent approach with all home/school problems. It also helps if you can honestly say something positive about the student.

BEHAVIOR

Letter Concerning Poor Behavior

Dear Mr. and Mrs. Harris:

As Jim's teacher, I am naturally concerned about his academic progress. Because I see in Jim a potential for achievement, I am also concerned about his personal growth and development. When I see something that I feel may interfere with that development, it is my duty to inform you of it and offer any services I may be able to provide to help Jim.

Over the past month, I have witnessed a change in Jim's behavior in school. It had first been confined to what some people would call mischievous, such as "cutting up" in class, placing a tack on another student's chair, and knocking over a pile of books. Lately, however, I have noticed him on the playground pushing and striking several smaller students. I have tried to speak with Jim on several occasions, but he does not offer any explanations.

I know you must be as anxious as I am to help Jim overcome this behavior. I have scheduled a conference for 2:30 P.M. on Thursday, November 8, in the main office of the school. I am certain that, working together, we can be of help to Jim.

If the time is inconvenient, please call the school and let me know what time would be best for you.

I look forward to meeting you.

Sincerely,

SPECIAL NOTE: Always maintain a positive approach when contacting parents about behavioral problems. Even if nothing comes of it, these written records indicate YOUR attempts at alleviating the problem.

Letter Concerning Good Behavior

Dear Mr. and Mrs. Byrne:

Too often our time at school is spent contacting parents about the negative behavior of their children. Thus, it is always a pleasure to be able to write a letter such as this one to express admiration for the positive behavior of a child.

It is a delight to have your son Josh in class. His thirst for knowledge, his inquisitiveness, and his quick mind make him a wonderful student; his kindness, unselfishness, helpfulness, and optimism make him an outstanding child. You certainly have every reason to be proud of him.

It is not unusual for a student to gain favor in the eyes of the faculty *or* in the opinion of the students, but when a child is so highly thought of by *both* faculty and students, it is a real accomplishment and shows a truly fine individual.

Josh is, indeed, a credit to you both.

Sincerely,

SPECIAL NOTE: It feels very good to be able to write such a letter. Too often we concentrate on the negative, so it does us good to sometimes remember some of the fine children we teach.

Letter Concerning the Use of Improper Language

To All Students:

Perhaps you have heard the saying, "There is a time and a place for everything." This means that something that may be all right at one time and in a certain place may not be all right or correct in another situation or at another time.

Lately, I have become aware of some students in the class who are using language that is not proper for school. You know what I am talking about. Whether it be called "vulgar" or "obscene," it is language that offends people.

Certainly, when you are alone or with other people who may not care if such language is used, you are free to use whatever language you choose. But if a person is offended by that language in school, he or she cannot just get up and walk away. Therefore, when you use such language in a public situation, such as school, you are hurting other people, and this no one should be allowed to do. Indeed, this is the reason why the school has a rule against the use of this language in the first place.

I know that I have only to bring this to your attention and you will see to it that the problem does not happen again. I think we all want our school and our room to be as pleasant as possible for everyone. Let's make every effort to keep it that way.

Sincerely,

SPECIAL NOTE: If you are really having a language problem, you might add a parental return slip to the bottom of this letter. When parents are made aware of a problem, it usually is reduced drastically.

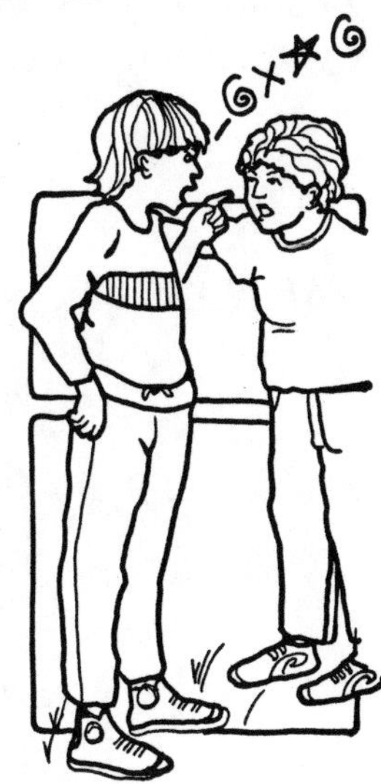

BOOKS

Request for Books for Class Library

Dear Parents:

STOP! Don't clean, don't straighten up, don't throw out another item until you have read this.

We are trying to start a class library. This is envisioned as a section of our classroom containing a large number of books of interest to your child and the other members of the class. If a child finishes his or her work a little early, prefers to spend some quiet time reading, needs a book for a report, or simply wishes to experience the joys of reading, these books would be available.

We have the space, we have the shelves—now all we need are the books. This is why we are turning to that traditional source of our strength: you, the parents.

If you have any books at home that are gathering dust or getting in your way, we would like to volunteer to give them a good home. Of course, the books should be appropriate for school use and of a reading and interest level suited to a sixth grade student. If you keep your own child in mind, you cannot go wrong.

All contributions will be gratefully accepted. If you have any questions, please do not hesitate to call me at the school. On behalf of all our students, thank you for your continued support.

Sincerely,

SPECIAL NOTE: We once saw this letter solicit enough books to start not one but three class libraries. Make certain, however, that you check every book that comes in for appropriateness.

CHEATING

Letter Concerning Student Caught Cheating

Dear Mr. and Mrs. Hendly:

I would like to tell you what I observed on the morning of January 22, 19xx. At this time, the students in my room were engaged in taking the district-wide mid-term exam in sixth grade English. I was proctoring this examination.

About 20 minutes into the examination, your son, John, raised his hand and asked to sharpen his pencil. I gave my permission for this, and, as he rose from his desk, he turned rather quickly, and I observed a number of index cards drop from under his sweater. John quickly bent to pick them up, and I went to help him, despite his protestations that he could get them and that I should "stay away." As I picked up several of the cards, John flushed deeply and loudly proclaimed that he had "found them on the floor" and "wasn't using them." A quick examination showed them to be outlines of the material being covered on the examination. A later examination and comparison to John's written classwork shows a substantial resemblance in handwriting. I took the cards and allowed John to complete the test. The corrected test indicates completely correct answers for the first three questions and incomplete or totally wrong answers on all subsequent questions.

I am concerned with one thing only—John's welfare, and I know that this must be your primary concern as well. Therefore, before I proceed further and before I make any decisions, I am most anxious to have your input and to share in your wisdom concerning John. I know that, working together, we can remedy any problem that John may be having.

May I count on you to call the school as soon as possible to arrange for a meeting? I know we can work this out.

I look forward to meeting with you.

Sincerely,

SPECIAL NOTE: You will notice that nowhere in this letter is John accused of cheating. Rather, only that which was directly observed is recounted, and the facts are allowed to speak for themselves. Notice also that there are no recriminations. Rather there is an honest appeal for the home and school to work together for the child's benefit. This is the type of letter that gets results.

CUTTING

Letter Concerning a Student Who Cuts Class

Dear Mr. and Mrs. Farrel:

Recently I had a talk with your son, David, concerning an incident that happened on Friday, May 3. On that date, Dave was absent from my class, although attendance records indicated that he was present in school that day.

When I confronted Dave with this fact, he admitted that he had, indeed, cut that class, which was the last period of the day. He further added that it was the first really warm day of spring, and he and several of his friends had decided that going fishing was an excellent idea. All of this David admitted freely and without prompting.

He further apologized for cutting the class and gave me his word that it would not happen in the future. I believe that he is sincere, and I am certain this will not happen again.

David understands that I am contacting you to inform you of what has happened.

Thank you for your understanding.

Sincerely,

SPECIAL NOTE: Informing the parents every time a student cuts class is an excellent idea. If it is a one-time offender, as the above letter seems to indicate, then it will do no harm. If the student becomes a repeat offender, then you will have a record of home notification and a basis for home/school cooperation in solving the problem.

DISCIPLINE

Form Letter Concerning Disciplinary Action

Dear ________________________:

I am sorry to report that your child, ____________________, a student in my class, was referred to the office by me for disciplinary action.

I referred ____________________ specifically for: ____________________

____

____

____

____

I am certain that you must be as concerned about this situation as I am. We all have ____________________'s interest at heart, and perhaps a conference might prove beneficial for all concerned.

If you will call the school, a convenient meeting time will be arranged. I look forward to meeting you.

Sincerely,

SPECIAL NOTE: Personally, we don't think a form letter is the best course of action with a disciplinary referral. Perhaps you might use this as a model in composing your own handwritten note. Save the form letter for those emergencies when you don't have time.

FIELD DAY

Informational Letter

Dear Parents:

On Friday, May 25, 19xx, we are holding our annual Field Day. Children should come dressed in casual play clothes suitable for the activities of the day.

On Field Day we will provide hot dogs and 12-ounce cans of fruit punch for the children if they wish to purchase the food.

We will be able to provide a maximum of *two* hot dogs and *two* cans of punch for each child. The prices are:

HOT DOGS:		PUNCH:	
	1—40¢		1—30¢
	2—80¢		2—60¢

NO HOT LUNCHES WILL BE SERVED ON FIELD DAY. Free milk, however, will be available for those students who normally receive the free lunch. Children wishing to purchase milk at 15¢ each container may do so. Children may also bring their own lunches.

Please send in the money for Field Day on Monday, May 21, 19xx. Since Field Day lunches will be handled separately, payment for regular lunches for the week of May 21 should include money for only four days instead of five days and will be collected on Friday, May 18. Thus, lunch payments are:

4 days—regular lunch	$3.60
4 days—reduced lunch	1.40
4 days—milk only	.60

Thank you for your cooperation in helping us to plan this activity.

Sincerely,

SPECIAL NOTE: If you have ever been in charge of a field day, then you already know that things will run a great deal smoother if everyone knows beforehand precisely what is expected. This applies to parents as well as students. A letter such as this one helps keep parents informed.

GRADUATION

Form Letter Concerning Graduates

Dear ________________________:

In a few short days, ____________________ will be graduating from ________________________________. As ____________________'s teacher for this year, may I extend to you my congratulations. ____________________ was a ____________ student in my class, and I have grown to like (him/her). I am certain that (he/she) will do well in life and will be a credit to you as (he/she) is now.

My best wishes for a happy future.

Sincerely,

SPECIAL NOTE: Do not use this as the "form" letter you see above. Rather, use it as an outline and hand write every note. This is one of the best devices for building community good will that there is. Remember, pleased parents pass budgets.

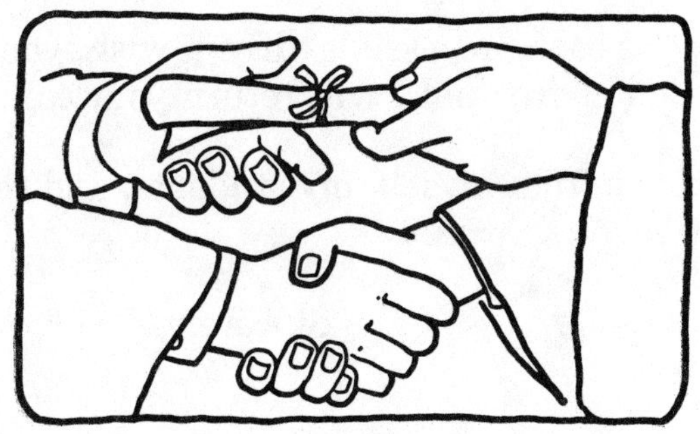

INSTRUCTION

Appeal to Business for Free Materials

Dear Mr. Farber:

As owner of the Farber Travel Agency, you have served this community for many years. Indeed, I have used your services and have been most pleased with the results.

I teach sixth grade at our local elementary school. Currently we are working on a project involving reports about cultures in countries around the world. These reports would be greatly enhanced and the children would learn a great deal if they had photographs and current information about these countries. The brochures that cover the walls of your agency would be ideal for use by my students in their current project.

Would it be possible for you to donate two or three of each brochure for our use in class? If so, I could arrange for either myself or one of our class parents to pick them up. Naturally, we would expect that your business logo would be on each one; the children would send you a letter of thanks, and a class letter sent to each parent would detail your contribution.

May I please know as soon as possible? If you wish, you may call me at the school's number listed above, and I will return your call very quickly.

Thank you in advance from myself, my students, and their parents for any and all considerations.

Sincerely,

SPECIAL NOTE: You are not asking for the free materials that many book and educational supply houses offer as a matter of course; rather, you are literally asking for a contribution from a local business. Consequently, you should offer something in return. Notice the implication is that the contribution will be made known to the parents, who will be impressed and use the services of this business. Since a business must do business in order to stay in business, your request is likely to be honored.

Appeal to Parents for Instructional Materials

Dear Parents:

While there are sufficient textbooks and classroom supplies for all our children, we are nevertheless constantly on the lookout for anything that we could use as an instructional aid. Therefore, I'd like you to know about and be on the lookout for:

Books— old encyclopedias (even incomplete sets); appropriate paperbacks; atlases; old textbooks.

Games—particularly word games; packs of alphabet cards; math-based games; mind games (concentration).

Items— models of things that work (engine, human eye, etc.); globes; maps; old microscopes; remnants of a chemistry set; old erector set; etc.

We will gladly accept these and any other items you decide could make good instructional materials. Remember, rather than throw it away, give it to us! Perhaps we can all benefit from such an exchange.

Thank you for your consideration.

Sincerely,

SPECIAL NOTE: You would be amazed at the amount of perfectly useable instructional material people throw away every day. If you can stockpile this material, you will find a fantastic resource.

Request for Guest Speaker

Dear Congressman Bailey:

As congressman for our district, I fully realize how busy you are and in what short supply your time must be. Certain, that time must be allotted to the duties of your office and the obligations of your position, and I am certain that little time remains for much else.

With that understanding, I am nonetheless respectfully requesting that you give some consideration to spending a few of those precious hours in an endeavor potentially beneficial to our state and to our nation. Namely, I am requesting that you become a teacher for approximately two hours.

Please allow me to explain. My sixth grade class has been studying the structure of our government as part of their curriculum. While they are working hard, I am sure that you will agree that there is no substitute for practical experience. I feel that even a short time spent with you, who has served the public for much of his adult life and who is intricately aware of the functioning of our democratic form of government, would be an enormous benefit to these children and an experience that they will remember forever.

If you will consider this request, there are several things you should know. We would be happy to accommodate your visit at your convenience at whatever time during the school year that your schedule would permit. We would arrange for you to speak to one class or the entire grade, whichever you prefer. We would arrange for press coverage of the event, and a letter would be sent home to the parents of every student detailing your contribution.

I thank you in advance for considering this request. If you cannot make it, we will certainly understand, but if you can find the time to honor this request, we know that you will find it a rewarding experience, and we know that our children will reap enormous benefits.

Sincerely,

SPECIAL NOTE: While this request is to a political figure, all requests for guest speakers should follow along these lines. Try not to set a specific date when the speaker must appear. Acknowledge that the speaker is a busy person, and allow him or her to choose the time. Keep the tone positive, assume cooperation, and make certain to offer something such as free publicity. Structured in these terms, your letter is likely to bring results.

NATIONAL HONOR SOCIETY

Letter of Congratulations

Dear Mr. and Mrs. Porter:

On behalf of myself and our entire class, may I extend our heartfelt congratulations on the election of your daughter, Pamela, to the National Honor Society. As I am certain you are aware, this honor reflects far more than merely Pam's academic achievement. Indeed, it is a testimony to her moral integrity, outstanding school citizenship, and constructive ideals. Everyone here knows that Pamela is truly deserving of this honor.

In a very real sense, your daughter's honor is yours as well. It is you who have provided the basis for the development of her character and the encouragement and support that have made her such an outstanding student and person.

You have our congratulations and our best wishes for every success in Pamela's bright future.

Sincerely,

SPECIAL NOTE: When the opportunity presents itself to say something positive to parents, we ought to take it.

OPEN HOUSE

Invitation to Attend (Example A)

Dear Parents:

I would be very pleased if you would accept an invitation.

On Wednesday, November 8, 19xx, as part of American Education Week, our school will be holding an Open House for all members of the community from 10:00 A.M. until 2:00 P.M. The entire school will be open for visitation, and I sincerely hope that you will be able to attend and visit our classroom and perhaps observe a lesson in which your child participates. Believe me, you would be a most welcome guest.

This day will provide you with an excellent opportunity to observe the place where your children spend such a great part of their lives.

I look forward to meeting you.

Sincerely,

SPECIAL NOTE: Take the initiative; invite the parents to your room before they get the official notice from the school. This active seeking of parental involvement will pay dividends in support should you ever have a problem.

Invitation to Attend (Example B)

Dear Parents:

We would like to invite you to our fifth grade Open House on Thursday, October 6, 19xx at 7:30 P.M. This will give us the opportunity to meet and inform you of our new programs, homework policy, and subject curriculum.

On a more personal note, this will enable us to open the lines of communication for the benefit of your child. Although teachers cannot be available for private conference at this time, please feel free to contact us in the near future if you feel a private conference is necessary.

Please return the slip below by Monday, October 3.

Sincerely,

Fifth grade teachers

Child's name ____

____ I will

____ I will not
be able to attend the Open House.

____
Parent's signature

SPECIAL NOTE: Although this letter is similar to the preceding invitation, it comes from a grade level. It includes a return slip so that you may anticipate the number of parents who will attend. Note that specific mention is made of the fact that no private conferences will be held.

PARENTAL CONTACT

Initial Contact Note

Dear ____________________:

Guess what? We have something in common! Namely, your child, ____________________. I have ____________________ in class this year, and I look forward to a year filled with learning and growth for ____________________. I also look forward to getting to know you better as the year progresses.

I believe that we must look upon ourselves as partners working together for a goal we both desire, namely, ____________________'s education and growth.

Let's look forward to a good year. But, if there are problems, let's both remember that as partners we have the same goal in mind and we can talk. I have your phone number from ____________________'s records, and I can always be reached through the school at 222-2222.

One more thing: ____

____

Here's to a good year!

Sincerely,

SPECIAL NOTE: This is a particularly good way to start off the year with a parent. It immediately establishes a nonthreatening rapport that could benefit you and your student later on. This is presented as a form that you would fill in with the child's name, etc. The section after "One more thing," should be filled in with a personal observation or comment, very personal in nature, about the child. A typical one might read, "Robert sits near a large, sunny window and has already told me about his dog, Bonnie." You could use this form as is, or you could use it as a model and write each one individually so it would look less like a form letter.

P.T.A.

Notice of Activity

Dear Parents:

On December 21, 19xx, River Road School had their Annual Student/Staff volleyball game. Many parents attended the event and enjoyed it so much that they thought it would be fun to have a Parent/Teacher volleyball game.

The challenge was accepted and the big game is scheduled for January 12, 19xx, from 7:30 to 10:00 P.M. in the River Road School gym.

In order to set up the game, we need to know how many parents will be participating. Please fill in the form below and return it with your child if you wish to play.

PLEASE REMEMBER TO WEAR SNEAKERS AND COMFORTABLE CLOTHING!

This event is for parents and teachers. There will be NO provisions for supervising children during the volleyball game.

Thank you. We are looking forward to seeing you on the 12th.

Sincerely,

River Road School Staff

PLEASE RETURN BY TUESDAY, JANUARY 10, 19XX

____ Yes, I will play in the Parent/Teacher volleyball game.
Parent's name ______________________________

SPECIAL NOTE: Notice the friendly and positive attitude conveyed by this letter. Such a note brings returns. The tone of this letter also helps establish good parent-teacher rapport and home-school communication.

Letter to Solicit Membership

Dear Parents:

The Thornton Junior High School P.T.A. invites you to become a member for the 19XX–19XX school year. Let us strive for 100 percent membership. Remember, the money from your dues is used for the benefit of your children.

Dues are $2 per person per year. Please indicated below the names of the people joining and the amount remitted. Return the slip below with your child to his or her homeroom teacher whether or not you are joining.

Sincerely,

Date ____________

I ( ) DO ( ) DO NOT want to join the P.T.A. for the current school year.

Name(s) ______________________________

____

Address ______________________________

____

Telephone number ______________ Amount enclosed ________

OPTIONAL: I volunteer to work on the following (for example, trip chaperone, baked goods, rummage collections and sales, etc.):

____

____

SPECIAL NOTE: As with the preceding letter, this is short and to the point, and will bring results.

READING

Informational Letter

Dear Mr. and Mrs. Perry:

If you have ever fixed a leaky faucet, built a bookcase, or repaired a car, then you know that in order to get the job done properly you must have the correct tools.

In a very real sense, the job of our children in school is learning. We know they must learn now in order to prepare themselves for the adult world as a functioning member of society. There is one "tool" that is essential if they are to accomplish this task, and that is the ability to read well. Without this essential tool, the job of learning becomes as frustrating as trying to cut a log in two without a saw.

Fortunately, our school has a complete program of reading instruction to help the child who is reading below grade level or who may have special problems with the reading process.

Recently your son, Tom, was referred to us, and subsequent testing has shown that he would benefit from our program. You will be advised of Tom's progress, and we look forward to a healthy improvement in Tom's reading ability.

If you have any questions, please feel free to contact the school. A conference may be arranged if you wish.

Yours sincerely,

SPECIAL NOTE: This letter would be one from the reading specialist to the parents. The teacher could well use parts of it to inform parents of a child's need for reading help or referral to the program.

Report on Child's Advancement in Reading

Dear Mr. and Mrs. Johnston:

I am happy to report that Brian has been advanced to the Level II reader. Research and experience have shown that a child has mastered one level and is ready for a higher one when he or she can:

1. Recognize 95 to 100 percent of the words;
2. Understand 75 to 100 percent of the content.

The reader Brian has mastered is being sent home so that your child can share with you some of the stories we enjoyed so much over the past few months.

Be a good listener. Sit down with your child. Let him pick the story or parts of stories he wants to read. Discuss the stories with him. Be generous with your praise.

If Brian is occasionally troubled by a word, ask him to read the rest of the sentence and see what word would make sense. Then, if he is still unable to get it, supply the word without comment and go on.

Look over the workbook together, too. You will be interested in the practice experience your child is getting.

I would appreciate your comments and questions at any time concerning your child's reading. Thank you for your cooperation.

Sincerely,

SPECIAL NOTE: This is a terrific letter to parents for several reasons. First, it is praise for their child and evidence that he or she is doing well. Next, it enlists their active participation in the child's education and opens doorways that you might find useful later. Finally, it teaches them how to deal with reading and their child. Try this one, and you'll find that you will like the positive results it brings.

RETENTION

Letter to Parents

Dear Mr. and Mrs. Dugan:

I know that by now you have received official notification from the school of the intention of retaining your daughter, Jeanne, in fourth grade for next year.

As you recall, this is a possibility that we discussed a number of times during conferences. Despite continued help by me and what I know has been a concentrated effort at home by you, Jeanne simply does not display a sufficient grasp of the material to allow her to be comfortable or successful in next year's fifth grade class. Rather than let her go on, only to meet with more frustration and failure, we felt that she should be retained now in order that she get a firm grasp on the knowledge she will need for later success.

Believe me, I will give Jeanne my every attention, and I have every hope for her success next year. If you have any questions, or if I may be of help in any way, please feel free to contact me at once.

Sincerely,

SPECIAL NOTE: The decision to retain a student does not come overnight, and it is well to remind the parents of this. Of course, it is only good sense that one be extremely gentle with the parents as well as pointing out the necessity for the retention.

SMOKING

Letter Concerning Student's Smoking

Dear Mr. and Mrs. Brown:

It is a rule of the school that any student caught smoking on school grounds must be sent to the office for disciplinary procedures. Therefore, when I discovered Shirley smoking on the playground, I had no choice but to observe the rules.

While I am certainly concerned with a breach of discipline, I am more concerned that Shirley is smoking; this, as we all know, is an unhealthy practice, especially for one so young. I have spoken to Shirley, and there is the possibility that she is smoking in order to please some of her peers. If this is the case, I believe that my talking with her, combined with your views expressed to her at home, might deter her from this practice.

Hopefully we can work together and try to dissuade Shirley from this practice in the future. If you have any questions, please contact me at the school.

Sincerely,

SPECIAL NOTE: Regardless of whether you smoke or not, none of us wants to see our children start the habit. Sometimes a good conference with the child and help from the home can go a long way toward solving the problem.

TARDINESS

Notification of Student's Tardiness

DATE: ____________________

Dear ______________________________:

This is to inform you that your son/daughter, ____________________, has been late to my class a total of __________ times during the period from ____________________ to ____________________.

I am certain that you know how important it is to be in class on time. Working together, I am sure that we can impress upon your child the necessity of being on time to class.

Please sign this form below and return it to me.

Thank you,

Teacher: ______________________________

Signature of Parent/Guardian: ______________________________

SPECIAL NOTE: It has been our experience that nothing clears up tardiness to class like a note home to the parents. This form assumes that you have kept good records, which you would undoubtedly do in your mark book or attendance book.

UNDERACHIEVEMENT

Report Concerning Student's Underachievement

Student ______________________ Grade ___ Marking Period Ends _____

Subject _______________ Teacher ______________________ Date _____

Dear Parents:

As your child's teacher, I am becoming concerned about a situation that is beginning to develop and that could have serious effects upon your child's school career if not handled soon. Therefore, I am sending you this report in the hope that, acting as a team, we may help your child's academic progress.

__________________ appears to be working at a level well *under* that which he/she could be. Based upon previous tests, written work, and personal observation, I believe that your child could be producing much better work than he/she is currently producing. I am sure you know that this could lead to poor grades and a lack of valuable skills on the part of your child should this trend continue.

I have checked below some of the actions your son/daughter might take in order to improve this situation. If you have any questions, or if you believe that a conference with all concerned parties might be helpful, please call me at the school to arrange a meeting.

___ be more attentive in class
___ be more cooperative in class
___ come prepared for class (bring books, pencil, etc.)
___ listen and follow directions carefully
___ participate more actively in class
___ learn to take notes in class
___ learn to accept criticism and evaluation
___ do the assigned work regularly (homework, classwork, etc.)
___ find out about and make up assignments after absences
___ try to improve the quality of assignments
___ study more diligently for tests and quizzes
___ respect the rights of others
___ come for extra help when needed
___ other:

Working together, we can help your child do the work he/she is capable of doing and bring his/her level of progress up where it should be.

Please sign this report and return it to me via your child. If you have any comments, please use the back of this report. Thank you for your understanding and cooperation.

Signature of Parent/Guardian ______________________________

Date ______________________________

SPECIAL NOTE: *"If only I had known" is a common cry in education. This report not only informs the parent of the underachiever, but also enlists support and gives specific direction for improvement.*

VOLUNTEERS

Request to Parents

Dear Parents:

As you know, May 17 is going to be a big day at our school. The annual Student Pet Fair is an activity traditionally well attended and is a favorite of students, parents, and faculty.

Some time ago, we sent a letter enlisting your support as volunteers for various Fair committees. We are happy to report that the response was overwhelming and every committee is filled—all, that is, except one.

As of this writing, the Cleanup Committee consists of one person—me. I am tempted to take my favorite Humphrey Bogart stance and say, "Sure it's a dirty job, but somebody has to do it." The reality, however, is simply this: I NEED YOUR HELP.

If I don't have someone to help, folks, it's going to take me until next July to get the place looking normal. If I can only convince one (or two or ten or twenty) of you to join me, I know it will go faster and we might even share a laugh or two along the way.

So, how about it? Will you help on this detail? Please give me a call at the school and I'll add your name to mine on the list.

I really will appreciate any help you may be able to offer.

Sincerely,

SPECIAL NOTE: When you do have a basically unpleasant task to get done, we have found that a little humor combined with blatant honesty goes a long way toward getting the volunteers you need. Parents will probably laugh at this letter, but they will also respond.

Soliciting Volunteer Workers

!! VOLUNTEERS NEEDED !!

The Parent-Teacher Association of Thornton Junior High School needs the support of ALL parents. If you can help out in any of the areas listed below, please indicate your interests. Participate in some way—the P.T.A. needs YOUR help.

( ) DANCE CHAPERONES (We need parents to chaperone one or more school dances held at various times throughout the school year.)

( ) LIBRARY (We need parents to work in the school library one afternoon until 3:30 P.M. every other week.)

( ) HEALTH OFFICE (We need parents to serve two hours per week typing and doing clerical work and perhaps giving a little TLC.)

( ) REFRESHMENTS (We need parents to bake for such school functions as Back-to-School Night and Arts Night.)

( ) TELEPHONING (We need parents to contact other parents by telephone for P.T.A. and other school-related functions.)

( ) RUMMAGE SALE COMMITTEE (Held in November, the rummage sale is our most successful fund raiser. We need parents to help organize and run this annual event.)

( ) DINNER DANCE COMMITTEE (We need parents to help organize and run this annual dinner dance given every June for our ninth-grade class.)

( ) P.T.A. EXECUTIVE BOARD (There are positions still open for anyone wishing to get involved. We meet every other Tuesday at 8:00 P.M. in the school library.)

( ) OTHER (If you wish to become involved and volunteer for something other than those activities described above, please indicate here.)

____

____

Name ____

Telephone ______________________ Best time to call __________

Name of child in school ______________________________

Grade ______________ Homeroom teacher ______________________

SPECIAL NOTE: *While this is a solicitation for volunteers for a P.T.A., the form can be adapted to whatever activity or purpose for which you need volunteers. If it is coming from you, you might want to personally sign the request.*

Letter of Thanks to Volunteers

Dear Volunteers:

Do you know what this is?

This is your medal for service above and beyond the line of duty. I only wish I had a real one, made of 24K gold, to give to each and every one of you. *You deserve it!*

I want you to know how much I appreciate the volunteer work you have done for our students and our school. You have given freely of your time, your unlimited energies, and your valuable expertise to make our project a success.

I have had many favorable comments from the faculty, the students, and other parents and community members who also appreciate your efforts.

You have my heartfelt gratitude for all that you have done!

Sincerely,

SPECIAL NOTE: This letter works! It may seem sentimental and even trite, but experience has shown us that the letter is very well received. We even know of someone who framed the medal and mounted it on a wall at home. Try to find the largest self-stick gold star you can and attach it to the medal. You'll receive many fine comments on this one.

Sign-up Sheet for Volunteers

THANK YOU FOR HELPING!

Please indicate below your name, telephone number, and exactly what you wish to do to help out. Thanks again for caring!

Name	Telephone	What Would You Like to Do?

SPECIAL NOTE: *This form can be used for any committee or project on which you need volunteer workers. Its advantage is that it requires people to write down what they will do and can serve as a check later on. Also, if this is passed around during an initial meeting, as people see what their neighbors are volunteering to do, they get an added incentive to volunteer themselves.*

WORK-STUDY PROGRAM

Letter Concerning Program

DATE: ________________

Dear ______________________________:

I would like your permission to recommend __________________ for placement in the work-study program currently being conducted at our school.

In this program, a student spends approximately half of the school day taking the normal required courses in school, and the other half working at a salaried position with a cooperating employer here within the Township.

I have found that this program can be of tremendous benefit to some students, providing them with maturity and experience in real-life situations.

This is a carefully monitored program, the details of which I am enclosing with this letter. Participation in this program requires your consent.

Please check and sign below, and return this paper to me.

Sincerely,

Student: ____ Date: ________________

( ) I grant my permission for you to recommend my child to the work-study program.

( ) I believe a conference would be helpful. Please arrange one and inform me of it.

( ) Other: ____

____

Signature of Parent/Guardian: ____

SPECIAL NOTE: It's not for every student, but for some, a work-study program can be beneficial. This form prepares parents for the possibility of their child's placement in one and opens the door to productive communications between the home and school.

Section 4

For Students

AWARDS

Letter to Award Recipient

Dear Sarah:

I want you to know how pleased I am that you are to receive our school's Outstanding Citizenship Award. As you probably know, this is a highly prized award that goes to the one student who has manifested the qualities of leadership, courage, kindness, and achievement.

This year, the faculty's job was all the easier because you were in our school! Your unselfish devotion to others, shown by your work on the Student Council, your high academic standing, and the high personal regard in which you are held by faculty and students alike, simply could not be denied. There is no doubt in anyone's mind that the Outstanding Citizenship Award is going to the right person.

Please accept my personal congratulations as well as the expression of my sincere pleasure in having you as a student this year.

Sincerely,

SPECIAL NOTE: What a joy it is to be able to write a letter like this one. All too often, attention is drawn to the "squeaky wheel," and you can forget or tend to overlook the good students who make the up the majority of your classes. Writing this type of letter benefits the student and you.

CHEATING

Letter Concerning Cheating

Dear John:

As you know, following the incident of the index cards during the midterm exam, I met with your parents. I am certain that they have spoken to you and expressed their concerns.

I have reserved Wednesday afternoon, January 30, after school in my room for a conference between you and me. At that time, I will be speaking with you about the incident. I will also be asking you a question that I want you to think about: What do you, John Hendly, intend to do to make up for that incident? This is very important and I expect you to be prepared with an acceptable answer.

I also want you to think about something else. None of us, neither your parents nor myself, would be the least bit worried about this if it were not for the fact that we care about you—we are concerned enough that we don't want to see you enter into a habit that could ruin your future.

I will see you on the afternoon of the 30th.

Sincerely,

SPECIAL NOTE: We have found that if a child is a "first timer" and not a hardened cheater, this approach works very well, certainly a great deal better than any berating and castigation. Often, the mere fact that someone is concerned enough about him or her has a highly beneficial effect on the student. This letter should be handwritten or typed by you.

NATIONAL HONOR SOCIETY

Letter to Elected Student

Dear Pamela:

My heartiest congratulations! Your election to the National Honor Society is a credit to yourself and our school. I want you to know that I feel it is well-deserved.

Over the past months, I feel that I have come to know you well. Indeed, I can think of no one more deserving of this honor. In our relationship, I have been privileged to see you exemplify those high standards of integrity, citizenship, and academic achievement that are the hallmark of the National Honor Society.

You should know that I am extremely proud to have you as a member of my class. May your future be bright and filled with the success you so richly deserve.

Sincerely,

SPECIAL NOTE: A student who is elected to the National Honor Society justly deserves the praise of his or her teachers. This letter or one like it quite often becomes a keepsake for the student who is so honored.

RECOMMENDATION

Letter for a Student

Dear Sir:

In reply to your request for a recommendation for Ann Marie Farley for summer employment with your organization, it is my pleasure to recommend her to you without reservation.

I have known Ann Marie for the past three years, and she has been a student in my class over the past year. I have found her to be bright, naturally inquisitive, responsible, and enthusiastic. She has attained top marks in my subject, and I know that she has carried a high honor roll average throughout the year in all of her classes.

She works without being pushed, helps out wherever she can, and takes responsibility for her actions. She has a dynamic and warm personality, a mark of which is the fact that she is extremely popular with faculty and students alike.

I think that you will be fortunate to have such a personable and competent young person in your employ.

Sincerely,

SPECIAL NOTE: As with a colleague, or any recommendation for that matter, you can make your personal opinion known, but base it on fact, and establish that you know the person in a capacity that allows you to judge professionally.

REPRIMAND

For a Severe Disciplinary Infraction

Dear James:

Today I had the sad task of referring you to the vice-principal for disciplinary action because of your behavior in the hallway directly outside my room. I saw you strike another student with a book. That other student received a cut over his left eye, and it is only by luck that the book did not hit the eye itself, injuring the student more seriously or even permanently.

This is not the first time I have had to intervene in a fight in which you were engaged. Indeed, I have had to warn you against hitting other students on eleven separate occasions since the beginning of the school year. On each of those occasions, I have pointed out to you the seriousness of your actions and the possible consequences. I have sent you personal letters on all of those occasions, reminding you in writing of the necessity of a change in your behavior in this regard. Still, I have witnessed no change nor evidence of a willingness to change. Now another student has been injured.

It is my hope that the vice-principal will be able to impress upon you the serious nature of your behavior. I think you are a capable student, and it disturbs me that you are behaving in a way that stops you from being all that you can be.

A copy of this letter will be sent to your parents along with a request for a conference with them. Hopefully, you will come to realize the seriousness of your behavior and show a needed change.

For the sake of your future, I hope that this can be done, for all further incidents of this nature will mean very serious consequences for you.

Sincerely,

SPECIAL NOTE: Notice that the tone of the note is one of trying to help the student you have referred for disciplinary action. Since a copy of this will be sent to the parents, mention has been made of previous letters to the student. Hopefully, you have kept a copy of them, which will serve as evidence of your willingness to help.

SCHOLARSHIP

Letter of Congratulations

Dear Bob:

I was so pleased to learn that you have been awarded the Landon Scholarship this year. If anyone is deserving of it, you certainly fit the bill. I have so often witnessed your dedication and hard work, and it is heartening to realize that all that work has paid off.

I am positive that your years at college will be as productive as the ones you have spent with us.

Again, Bob, congratulations on an award richly deserved.

Sincerely,

SPECIAL NOTE: This is short and to the point. It is another example of acknowledging the positive rather than always concentrating on the negative.

SMOKING

Warning Note

TO ALL STUDENTS:

Is a person bad because he or she smokes? Of course not. Some of your parents or other relatives may smoke—and they are good people. Many of them started to smoke when very little was known about how dangerous smoking can be for your health. Smoking causes heart disease and lung cancer. Heart disease killed many Americans last year.

We know what smoking can do. Therefore, we owe it to ourselves and to the younger children who may be influenced by us to not start smoking. If someone you know wants to quit, you can help by being understanding. You can help yourself by NEVER starting.

If someone offers you a cigarette, you can be strong in your beliefs; you can be polite; but, be sure to say NO!

SPECIAL NOTE: It is important that you do not equate smoking (a bad habit) with bad people, as many parents may smoke. Our aim is to keep students from starting. Write to the Department of Health and to the American Cancer Society for their many free books and pamphlets on the subject.

STUDENT COUNCIL

Letter to Members

Dear Student Council Members:

As we draw near to the end of this current school year, I would like you to know that I appreciate the hard work and effort you have put into working for the improvement of our school over the past year.

As members of the Student Council, you have the satisfaction of knowing that you have served your classmates and your school through activities that have benefited everyone. You are a credit to our school.

I am proud to teach in a school with a Student Council the caliber of ours. Congratulations on a job well done.

Yours sincerely,

SPECIAL NOTE: This would be a fine letter to send if you were the faculty advisor to this group or merely as an individual to acknowledge the efforts of a group of good kids. It will be appreciated.

SYMPATHY

Letter for a Student

Dear Mr. and Mrs. Parsons:

I was very proud to have Karen as a student in my class. She was a bright young lady with a bubbling personality who was always there to help when she was needed. In all my years of teaching, Karen is one of a handful of students whose memories shall always remain with me.

I am deeply saddened by her passing, and my heart goes out to you. I wish to convey to you the sense of loss and deep sympathy felt by her classmates and other faculty members who were fortunate enough to know her. We shall miss her deeply.

If I may be of service in any way, I hope you know that I would consider it an honor. You need only ask.

With deepest sympathies,

SPECIAL NOTE: Death can be a tragedy at any age, but it seems particularly poignant when it happens to a young person. Here, again, merely say what you feel in an honest and open manner, and you will do fine.

TARDINESS

Message to Students

TO ALL STUDENTS:

There are a million reasons why someone could be late coming to class. You might run into "traffic jams" in the hallway; a teacher might ask you to run an errand; you may have simply lost track of time. No one could blame you for being late—once in a great while.

Indeed, if it happens once, with a good reason attached to it, nothing will be said. If, however, it becomes a habit or happens so frequently that you are beginning to lose class time, then something will have to be done.

That "something" may be anything from detention to involvement of your parents or the main office, depending upon the severity of your tardiness.

If a teacher detains you, then that teacher will give you a late pass. Otherwise, it is expected that you will be in your seats when attendance is taken directly after the passing bell sounds.

If you are conscientious, do what is expected of you, and make an effort to cooperate, there should be no difficulty with this necessary rule.

SPECIAL NOTE: Rules are particularly enforceable if they are reasonable and specifically spelled out for students. The message above provides students with specific direction for this rule against tardiness.

TEXTBOOKS

Message Concerning Care of Books

TO ALL STUDENTS:

Your textbooks are lent to you by this school in order that you may learn and receive an education. In almost all cases, these books are used from year to year as new students enter this class. Therefore, you should take particular care to preserve them and keep them as useable as possible.

When you received your textbook, its condition was indicated on the front inside cover. When the books are collected at the end of the school year, it is expected that the condition of the textbook will not have changed more than a year's normal use would indicate. If there is any damage done to your textbook during your possession of it, then you will be expected to pay for that damage or pay for a new book should yours be lost or defaced beyond use.

Therefore, it is your responsibility to keep your book covered and report immediately any vandalism or unusual circumstances regarding your textbook.

Sincerely,

SPECIAL NOTE: Here, again, sensible rules are spelled out very clearly for the student. Also, this notice is proof that the student could not have misunderstood what you said.

UNDERACHIEVEMENT

Warning Letter

Dear Gary:

Almost half of the marking period has passed and I have a problem. Frankly, that problem is you. I look at your grades in my marking book and then I think of what I know about you, and the two do not make sense.

When I think of you, I see an intelligent, likeable person who is more than capable of doing the work in this class and doing it well. But when I look at your grades, I see someone who is on the brink of failure and definitely producing far below his capacity. I just don't understand.

If only I could get inside your head and tell you that you are a student who could do outstanding work and who could get very good marks. If only I could convince you that with a little effort on your part, all these difficulties could disappear. If only I could tell you how worried I am that you are cheating yourself out of your future. I wish I could do these things.

What about it, Gary? Will you let me help you help yourself? You can do it. Will you make the effort? Will you get back on course so you can have a successful future?

The choice is yours, Gary. I hope you will choose wisely.

With great concern,

SPECIAL NOTE: With the underachiever, you are not working with the child who can't do the work. Rather, you are working with a capable student who won't do it. Sometimes, a "shocker" letter such as this one, in which your concern is evident, will have a dynamic effect.

YEARBOOK

Letter to Yearbook Staff

Dear Members of the Yearbook Staff:

The Yearbook is in, waiting in the stock room to be distributed to the school in a few days. This is the culmination of a very great task begun by you back in September of last year. In a short time, the entire school will witness the results of your considerable efforts.

And what an effort it was! I have been faculty advisor on a number of yearbooks, and I have seen no one surpass you for your dedication, hard work, and general competence. Your cooperation and devotion to an often frustrating and thankless task are deeply appreciated by me, personally, as they will be by the school population once they see the magnificent volume you have prepared.

Please accept my congratulations on a job well done. I am proud of each and every one of you!

Sincerely,

SPECIAL NOTE: A letter of thanks or appreciation is always welcomed by anyone who has worked hard. This letter, as you can surmise, is sent from the Yearbook Advisor to the members of the staff, although you may wish to send a private letter to your editors.

PART II

Forms

Section 1

For Parents

DETENTION

Notification Form

Dear ______________________________:

Your son/daughter, ____________________, has been assigned detention after school on ______________________________ because:

( ) Lessons poorly prepared or not done
( ) Inattention in class
( ) Work not done on time
( ) Unsatisfactory test score
( ) Poor attitude in class
( ) Absenteeism
( ) Frequently unprepared (without books, pencil, etc.)
( ) Disciplinary infraction: ____
____
( ) Other: ____
____
____

The detention period lasts 45 minutes after the close of school. If you have any questions, please feel free to call me at the school.

Date: ________________ Teacher: ______________________________________

SPECIAL NOTE: Send this home EVERY TIME a child gets detention, and you'll soon find the student having less and less detentions to worry about.

KINDERGARTEN

Checklist for Readiness

Child's Name: ______________________________

Child's Date of Birth: ______________________________

Please check what applies to your child:

( ) Toilet trained
( ) Feeds self
( ) Needs help feeding self
( ) Eats almost all foods
( ) Eats very few foods
( ) Has temper tantrums
( ) Teases other children
( ) Overactive
( ) Highly excitable
( ) Timid and/or shy
( ) Plays well with others
( ) 'Picked on' by others
( ) Overly aggressive
( ) Cries easily
( ) Has many fears
( ) Has few interests
( ) Has many interests
( ) Is attentive
( ) Cares for own property
( ) Follows requests
( ) Initiates own actions
( ) Speech impediment (explain)
( ) Does not speak (explain)
( ) Speaks in sentences
( ) Seldom speaks
( ) Speaks understandably

Use the back of this paper to explain if necessary.

My child needs to:
( ) Become self-reliant
( ) Get interested in something
( ) Become cooperative
( ) Adjust to other children
( ) Acquire manual/motor skills
( ) Relax
( ) Become more active
( ) Become less active
( ) Other: ______________________________

Comments: ______________________________

____

Signature of Parent/Guardian: ______________________________

Date: ______________________________

SPECIAL NOTE: This form allows the kindergarten teacher to know the concerns and expectations of the parent. It also allows parents to have a say in their child's education and appreciate the kindergarten teacher's concern.

SAFETY PATROL

Permission Form

Safety Patrol Permission Form

To Parents or Legal Guardians:

Your son/daughter wishes to be a member of our safety patrol. Parents are required by law to assume the responsibility for consenting to participation and to risk the liability of injury.

6:29–5.3 SAFETY PATROLS

A pupil desiring to serve on a school safety patrol or with any similar organization performing patrol duties shall file with the school principal a signed application form and a form of consent signed by one parent or legal guardian. The forms shall be provided by the board of education and they shall be worded in a manner to indicate that the applicant and his/her parent or guardian are aware of the possible hazards of patrol duty and that in case of injury to himself (herself) no liability shall be attached to the board of education or to any employee of the board of education.

Please sign your name at the bottom of this form if your child has your permission to be a member of our safety patrol.

I acknowledge that physical hazards may be encountered in the conduct of being a member of the safety patrol.

I waiver all claims for damages, remuneration, reimbursement or any other expense in case of personal injury, in conduct of the programs and in all arrangements incidental thereto.

Date ________________ Signature of Student ______________________________

Date ________________ Signature of Parent ______________________________

SPECIAL NOTE: Participation in a safety patrol activity can be a valuable experience for students. If you are in charge of one, however, it is wise to cover yourself and the school with a release.

SUGGESTIONS

Field Trip Suggestion Form

Dear Parents:

I could use your input. Throughout the school year, we like to take our students on field trips to places where they will learn something and have a good time as well. Understandably, the place must be relatively inexpensive and within a single day's travel there and back.

Do you have some ideas? If you do, I would really appreciate hearing them. Please use the form below and return it to me via your child. Any suggestions will be appreciated.

Thank you,

My suggestion for a field trip is:

Signature: ______________________ Date: ______________________

SPECIAL NOTE: You would be surprised not only at how many of these forms are returned, but also at the number of FREE trips to very interesting places that are arranged by parents who simply have never been asked for their suggestions before. Try it and you'll see.

VISION

Notice of Difficulties

Dear ______________________________:

Your child, ____________________, has been having some difficulties in class that may possibly be related to a vision problem.

Specifically, ____

____

____

____

Good vision is an essential part of your child's school career. I bring this to your attention, as I am positive you will wish to attend to this matter.

Please sign the form below and return it to me via your child.

Thank you,

Teacher: ________________________

- -

Date: ______________________________:

I have read the notice concerning a POSSIBLE vision problem my child may be having.

Name of Student: ____________________________ Grade: ______________

Signature of Parent/Guardian: ____________________________________

SPECIAL NOTE: Not only are you helping a child by sending home this form, but the return slip stands as evidence of your concern as well as of the fact that you have done your job. Having it returned also precludes the fact that some children, not wanting to wear glasses, might throw away such a notice.

Section 2

For Students

ACHIEVEMENT

Certificate

THORSON JUNIOR HIGH SCHOOL

____

has been awarded this certificate
in recognition of

OUTSTANDING ACHIEVEMENT
in

____

and particularly for

____

____

Awarded this _____ day of ___________________________, 19 _____

Teacher: ____

Principal: ____

SPECIAL NOTE: Everyone likes awards, especially students and their parents. While the above example is simple, it serves its purpose, allows for an individualized comment, and may be typed up easily on a ditto master for a ready supply.

BULLETIN BOARDS

Suggestion Form

TO ALL STUDENTS:

An attractive bulletin board not only makes our classroom a nice place to be, but it can also teach us about new and interesting things, display our work, or be a tool to use in our studies.

I am very interested in any suggestions YOU may have for future bulletin board displays in our room. (For example: The Most Dangerous Job in the World; Higher Education; Books We Have Loved; etc.) Please take a moment to complete the following form and place it in the tray on my desk.

Thank you for your suggestions.

My name is ______________________________ Date ______________

I think a good idea for a bulletin board would be:

____

____

____

____

I volunteer to do the following:

____

____

____

____

SPECIAL NOTE: This form and the next one should be used together. As you know, it would be counterproductive to elicit suggestions and then not act on them.

Responsibility Form

TO ALL STUDENTS:

Thank you for your suggestions for possible bulletin board displays. The following list was made from your suggestions and includes the names of those students who volunteered to help. Please take note of the dates assigned. I know you will do a great job. Let me know if I can be of any help.

DATE	THEME	VOLUNTEERS
October	______________________	______________
	______________________	______________
November	______________________	______________
	______________________	______________
December	______________________	______________
	______________________	______________
January	______________________	______________
	______________________	______________
February	______________________	______________
	______________________	______________
March	______________________	______________
	______________________	______________
April	______________________	______________
	______________________	______________
May	______________________	______________
	______________________	______________
June	______________________	______________
	______________________	______________

PLEASE NOTE: Volunteers are responsible for maintaining their bulletin board through their assigned month.

SPECIAL NOTE: This form, when used in conjunction with the form that follows, gives students a very proprietary feeling about the class bulletin board. We have found that when something is "theirs," vandalism and grafitti are kept to a minimum.

CALENDAR

Monthly Activity Calendar

Teacher: ______________________ Homeroom: ______________________

for the month of

______________________, 19 ______

DATE	ACTIVITY

SPECIAL NOTE: *While this form is set up for class activities, there is no reason why it could not be amended for special projects or assignments due. Forms of this type, posted prominently in the room, help children to develop self-reliance as they learn to check things for themselves rather than constantly relying on you.*

CITIZENSHIP

Certificate

THORNTON JUNIOR HIGH SCHOOL
be it known that

____

of the _____ grade
has exhibited

OUTSTANDING CITIZENSHIP

throughout the school year and is a credit to
the home, the school, and the community.

Awarded this _______ day of ______________________________, 19_______
Principal: ____
Teacher: ____

SPECIAL NOTE: Both students and parents love award certificates such as this one. They don't have to be printed on gold-edged stock. Even something simple, such as the form above, will be cherished.

Nomination Form for Award

Name ______________________________________ Date ______________

DIRECTIONS: Each year an award is given out in each class for outstanding citizenship. This award should go to the person in our class who has exhibited the traits of a good citizen: helpfulness, kindness to others, respect for other people, dependability, truthfulness, and all those qualities that make a person a good citizen—someone upon whom you can depend for help and someone who is good to have as a member of our class.

Please think for a moment and then write down the name of one person in our class whom you feel deserves the award. Also, briefly tell me why you believe this person should be nominated. I will be the only person to see your papers.

I think the Outstanding Citizenship Award should go to:

____

This person deserves this award because ___________________________

____

____

____

____

SPECIAL NOTE: It is always wise to allow your students to have a controlled say in the procedures and dealings of the class. Most students are honest and usually come up with the same name YOU would have chosen had you done it alone.

COMPLAINTS

Complaint Form

Name: ______________________ Date: __________

Complaint: (Describe your complaint as fully as possible. Remember that facts and not opinions are important.)

____

____

____

Suggestion: (In your opinion, what could be done to remedy the situation you describe above. Please be specific. No complaint will be read unless this section is filled out.)

____

____

____

Signature of Student: ______________________

SPECIAL NOTE: Notice that the student is free to complain IF he or she states facts rather than opinions and IF he or she can also supply a manner of remedying the situation. This very fact insures that any complaints you get will be serious in nature.

CONGRATULATIONS

General Form

Date: ______________________

Student: ____

You are to be congratulated for ______________________________

____

____

____

____

Keep up the good work!

Teacher: ____

SPECIAL NOTE: *You can get two of these forms to a ditto master and run them off in quantity. Thereafter, when a student has done something good in class, it takes but a second to provide that student with a tangible reinforcement of that good and positive behavior.*

EXTRACURRICULAR ACTIVITIES

Identification Card

THORNTON JUNIOR HIGH SCHOOL
This is to certify that

____

is a member of
THE THORNTON STAMP AND COIN CLUB
for the school year

19________–19________

Advisor: ______________________ Date: ____________

SPECIAL NOTE: This can be typed several times on a ditto master, run off on heavy paper or posterboard, and cut apart. Each card adds a sense of importance to the club you sponsor. When we first did this, no other club gave out ID cards to members. Now, they all do.

Interest Form

Name of Student: ______________________________

Grade: ______________ Homeroom: ______________

Homeroom Teacher: ______________________________

I am interested in the following activity(ies):

( ) NEWSPAPER	( ) STAMP AND COIN CLUB
( ) DRAMA CLUB	( ) CHESS CLUB
( ) YEARBOOK	( ) MODEL-MAKING CLUB
( ) TWIRLERS	( ) PEP CLUB
( ) CHEERLEADERS	( ) AUTOMOTIVE CLUB
( ) FRENCH CLUB	( ) MODERN DANCE CLUB

* * * * *

( ) Please send me information

( ) Please send me an application form

Date: ______________ Signature: ______________________________

SPECIAL NOTE: If you are ever in the position of acting as coordinator of student activities, have this form distributed throughout the building during the first few days of the school year. The respondents can then be directed to the proper faculty advisors. Incidentally, the bit about the "application form" lends an aspect of importance and selectivity to these extracurricular activities, even though everyone who applies gets in!

FAILURE

Student Notification

Dear ______________________________:

I am very sorry to have to tell you this, but my records show that you are not doing satisfactory work in (subject) ____________________ for the current marking period, which ends on ____________________. If this situation does not improve, you may fail.

In order to improve, you must:

( ) Come to class prepared with all necessary materials.

( ) Hand in assignments regularly and on time.

( ) Improve the quality of your assignments.

( ) Find out about missed assignments and tests and make them up.

( ) Give your complete attention to the explanations and practice exercises we do in class.

( ) Study harder and pass more tests.

( ) Improve your behavior in class.

( ) Come to me for extra help.

( ) Complete a major project.

( ) Other: ____
____

If I may help you in any or all of these, I will. I want you to succeed. Please have this form signed by your parent/guardian and returned to me by ____________________.

Date: ________________ Teacher: ______________________________

I HAVE READ THE ABOVE REPORT
SIGNATURE OF PARENT/GUARDIAN: ______________________
Date: ______________________

SPECIAL NOTE: The great advantage of this form is that it places responsibility directly onto the student. The return slip at the bottom also insures that the parents are aware of the situation as well.

GOALS

Individual Goal Form

When you set a goal for yourself, you have something to work for. You can then plan effectively how to obtain *your* specific goal. Take some time, give it some thought, and fill out the following form:

My goal for this year is: ______________________________

____

To obtain this goal, I plan to: ______________________________

____

My goal for all my schooling is: ______________________________

____

To obtain this goal, I plan to: ______________________________

____

My goal for my life is: ______________________________

____

To obtain this goal, I plan to: ______________________________

____

SPECIAL NOTE: This form does two things: first, it forces a student to think about what he or she wants out of school and how school will play a part in that, and second, it is a marvelous device to use as a basis for discussion or for informal counseling.

GRADES

Personal Grade Form

Student: ______________________________

Marking Period: ______________ Date: ______________

Subject: ______________________________

For this marking period, you earned
a grade of

_____

Comment: ______________________________

____

____

____

Teacher: ______________

SPECIAL NOTE: If you desire, you could write a parent verification notice at the bottom, having it signed and returned to you. You might want to give out this form as well as the standard report card, particularly if you wish to make a significant comment.

HALL MONITORS

Report Form

Name: ______________________________ Date: ______________

Area Monitored: ____

Time Monitored: From __________________ to __________________

Any unusual or disruptive incidents: ________________________

____

____

Students using hall passes (Please list):

____

____

____

____

Comments: ____

____

____

SPECIAL NOTE: Many teachers act as the heads of safety patrols or hall monitors. This form lends a sense of importance to the task, allows the student to feel that he or she is doing a valuable job, and may serve as an important document in the event of any real trouble in the halls.

HONOR ROLL

For a Class

Be it known that for the week of ______________________________ the following student(s) are recognized as outstanding and their names are placed on this special

CLASS HONOR ROLL

Student(s): ____

Reason: ____

____

____

____

Teacher: ____

SPECIAL NOTE: *Make up this form in bulk and display a new one each week. Add a touch of glitter or use metallic pens to write the students' names. Selection for this honor can be on whatever basis you choose, such as involvement in quiz scores, kindness shown to classmates, telling the truth when a lie would have gotten the child out of trouble, etc. You should be able to see to it that every child in your room gets on the list at least once.*

IDEAS

Good Ideas Sheet

TO ALL STUDENTS:

If you have a good idea that would help in the running of the class, I would like to know about it. Please use the form below, and return it to me.

Your name: ______________________________ Date: ____________

State your idea: ____

____

____

Explain how this idea would help our class: ______________________

____

____

____

____

____

____

SPECIAL NOTE: This is another device that allows students to feel they have a positive say in determining their environment. Notice it is phrased so that the student must have thought out the idea thoroughly.

LEADERSHIP

Evaluation Form

Student ____________________ Date __________

Grade __________ Activity __________ Homeroom __________

After each quality, place an X in the appropriate box.

QUALITY	NEVER	SOMETIMES	ALWAYS
initiates own actions			
accepts responsibility			
admits mistakes			
makes logical decisions in class			
demonstrates ability to handle pressure well			
gains peer acceptance honestly			
follows through on decisions			
is conscientious			
displays sensitivity to others			

Overall Performance ____________________

____

Recommendations ____________________

____

____

Evaluator's Signature ____________________ Date __________

SPECIAL NOTE: This is the type of form you might use in an athletic or other extracurricular activity to spot leadership potential in students. Of course, you could use it in the classroom as well.

LOCKERS

Individual Assignment Sheet

Date: ____________________

Student: ____

Your locker assignment for the 19________–19________ school year is:

Locker number: ____

Location: ____

Key number: ____

Please memorize this information, especially the key number, as soon as possible. Any difficulties with the locker or key should be reported to me immediately.

Teacher: ____________________

SPECIAL NOTE: We prepare this form before the school year starts, tape the key to the bottom of the note, and place it on the incoming student's desk. It is a tremendous timesaver on that first day of school when everything is so hectic.

MEDICAL PROBLEMS

Medical Excuse and Reassignment Form

Student: ______________________________ Date: ______________

Grade: ______________________________ Homeroom: ______________

The above-named student is excused from physical education and all physical activities for the period

from ______________________ to ______________________

Reason: ____

____

Confirmed by: ____

Student reassigned to: _________________________________

____

Comments: ____

____

Signature of teacher: __________________________________

SPECIAL NOTE: Confirmed medical excuses from physical activity are often handled through the school nurse. In many schools, however, the teacher must handle this. The above form is a convenient way of dealing with excuses and contains all the necessary information.

RECOGNITION

Certificate

CERTIFICATE OF RECOGNITION

This certifies that

____

has been awarded this certificate for participation in

____

____
SUPERINTENDENT OF SCHOOLS

__________________ __________________
P T A PRESIDENT PRINCIPAL

____

SPECIAL NOTE: Run this off on a copier, and you have a very official-looking certificate that is bound to impress students and their parents. Your name would go on the bottom line, and you can fill in the signatures of the others—with their permission, of course. OR have the other actually sign several certificates at one time.

SELF-EVALUATION

Student Form

What kind of student are you? For each of the following items, place an X in the box that best describes YOU.

	ITEM	ALWAYS	MOSTLY	SOMETIMES	NEVER
1.	I pay attention in class				
2.	If I do not understand, I ask.				
3.	I write down directions for assignments.				
4.	I take notes on what we study.				
5.	I do all my homework and assignments.				
6.	I study for tests and quizzes.				
7.	I work well alone or with others.				
8.	I volunteer to help when I can.				
9.	I start my work without having to be told.				
10.	I review what I have learned in class.				

SPECIAL NOTE: We distribute this form about the middle of the first marking period, allow a few minutes to have it completed, and then spend the rest of the class period discussing it and interpreting why each item is the mark of a good student. We have had very positive results from this activity.

SPORTSMANSHIP

Acknowledgment

Good Sports
are winners
even when
they lose.
___________was
a good sport!
Date
Signature

SPECIAL NOTE: *Winning is NOT the most important thing we teach in school, is it? Teaching the VALUES of good sportsmanship is just as important. A certificate such as this, which acknowledges those values, goes a long way toward inculcating them in our students. This form can be easily reproduced by machine. We suggest you keep a stack handy!*

STUDY

Independent Study Record

____________________'s Independent Study Record

Date	INFORMATION TO BE LEARNED	SKILLS TO BE PRACTICED	TEACHER'S COMMENTS	STUDENT'S COMMENTS

SPECIAL NOTE: This is a form easily typed on a ditto master and run off in quantity. It might be used as seen above for older students, or you might want to prepare it sideways on a ditto master, printing the titles of each column and illustrating it with art work for younger students. Either way, it is a good method of recording student independent study.

SUGGESTIONS

Student Form

Name: ______________________________ Date: ______________

Homeroom: ______________________ Grade: ______________________

In the space below, please write any suggestion you may have for the *improvement* of our class. Unsigned suggestions *will not be read.* All suggestions *must* be within the realm of possibility.

____

____

____

____

____

Signature of Student: ______________________________________

SPECIAL NOTE: If your students know that only signed suggestions get read by you, the practical-joke type will soon disappear. This way, students feel they have a say in their class, and you may get some really good suggestions.

TEXTBOOKS

Financial Obligation Form

Date of This Notice: ______________________________

Student: ______________________ Grade: __________

Homeroom: __________________ Subject: ______________

Textbook: ____________________________________

Amount of Fine Assessed: ________________________

Reason for Assessment of Fine: ___________________

____

Signature of Teacher: ________________________

SPECIAL NOTE: Here you have all the information needed for the assessment of a fine for abuse of the textbook. It is wise to have a copy of this in your files for each fine assessed. You might also consider having the student sign the original and the copy as proof that he or she was notified.

Section 3

For Teachers

ADDRESSES

Student Address Card

Please fill out *ALL* information on this card.

Name: ______________________________ Tel. No.: ______________

Address: ____

____

Where can your parents/guardians be reached during school hours (telephone number)?

Mother: ____________________ Father: ____________________

Best time to call home after school hours: ______________________

List the name and telephone number of a neighbor, friend or relative who lives close to you.

Name: ____

Relationship: ______________________ Tel. No.: ______________

SPECIAL NOTE: Something as simple as this card can save you hours of frustration. When you know when to call and where to reach someone who will inform parents of your call, much time and energy are saved.

Class List of Addresses

Teacher: ______________________ Grade or Subject: ______________

Period: ______________________ School Year: 19______–19______

Date Last Updated: ______________________________________

STUDENT	ADDRESS	TEL. NO.

SPECIAL NOTE: A list like the one above is extremely useful throughout the school year, especially since the telephone numbers are available at a glance. Run off this form on a ditto, and you will have more than enough for several school years.

BULLETIN

Weekly Class Bulletin

MRS. POTTER'S CLASS
Weekly Bulletin for the week of

____

This week's assignments:

Windows	Blackboard	Paper and Books
______	______	______
______	______	______
Cleanup	**Art Supplies**	**Homework Collection**
______	______	______
______	______	______

Special Projects:

____

____

Dates to Remember:

____

____

Birthdays this Week:

____

____

Thought for the Week:

____

____

SPECIAL NOTE: You would, of course, personalize this form to your specific classroom needs. It can be easily run off in quantity and displayed each week on the bulletin board. Students quickly learn to consult the bulletin for their assignments rather than constantly plague you with the same old question: What's the next assignment?

BUS

List for Class Trip

CLASS TRIP ROSTER

Teacher: ______________________ Date of Trip: ______________

Time of Departure: ______________ Time of Return: ______________

Method of Transportation: ______________________________

Destination: ______________________________________

The following students will be going on the trip at the date and times indicated above. They understand that it is their responsibility to make up any work done during their absence. Thank you for your cooperation and understanding.

STUDENT	Home Room	STUDENT	Home Room

SPECIAL NOTE: The completed form above is meant to be distributed to the faculty and staff of your school a few days before the actual date of the trip. This gives faculty and staff members a chance to "work around" the absent students. This same form may be used by you as a check-off list for bus attendance.

CHILD STUDY TEAM

Form for Quick Referral

EMERGENCY PRIORITY!

TO: Dr. Ellen Caulfield, Director, Child Study Team
FROM: Mrs. H. Donnelly, Teacher, Sixth Grade
RE: Emergency Referral

The following student has exhibited behavior which concerns me deeply. I feel, in my professional judgment, that this child may pose a potential threat to himself or others. I respectfully request that you see this child as soon as possible on a priority basis. I shall fill out all forms necessary at your request, but I feel that this child should be seen by you at once.

Date: ______________________________

Child's Name: ______________________________

Grade: ______________ Homeroom: ______________________________

Grade: ______________ Homeroom: ______________________________

Observed Behavior: ______________________________

____

____

____

____

____

Thank you for your *prompt* attention to this matter.

SPECIAL NOTE: We have found that one of the frustrations of teaching involves having to go through massive paperwork to get help for a child who needs help NOW! This form is something that cannot be ignored. Be sure to keep a dated copy for your files.

CLEANUP

Checklist

Thank you for volunteering for the clean-up detail. Please use the following checklist:

( ) Tables cleared
( ) Perishables stored
( ) Garbage bagged
( ) Supplies stored
( ) Floors cleaned
( ) Chairs rearranged
( ) Electrical plug disconnected
( ) Windows locked
( ) Doors locked
( ) Lights out
( ) Keys returned
( ) Decorations taken down
( ) Found items stored
( ) Final check of room

SPECIAL NOTE: A checklist such as this or one tailored to your specific needs saves a great deal of time and gets the job done thoroughly, particularly when you have put students in charge of the detail.

CONFERENCE

Checklist

Teacher: ______________________________ Date: ______________

Conference Concerning: ______________________________

This is the ______________ conference of the current school year.

People in Attendance: ______________________________

____

____

Points Discussed: ______________________________

____

____

Parental Reaction: ______________________________

____

____

Suggested Course of Action: ______________________________

____

____

General Comments: ______________________________

____

____

____

SPECIAL NOTE: Reproduce this form in quantity. Thereafter, make out a separate form for each conference that you hold. Do it while the conference is still fresh in your mind. If necessary, this is excellent proof of your attempts to help.

Log of Parents Not Attending

LOG OF PARENTS NOT ATTENDING PARENT CONFERENCES

Parent's Name	Scheduled Conference Date	Contacted by Note		Phone	No. of Times Contacted	1	2	3	4

SPECIAL NOTE: A visible record of contact and solicitation to come for a conference can be very helpful should you ever be faced by irate parents who charge that they would have done something "if only we had known." At the very least, this is a clear record of your attempts to help.

Parent-Teacher Conference Record

PARENT-TEACHER CONFERENCE RECORD

Student ______________________ Conference Date ______________

Teacher ______________________ Grade ______________

NOTE: A plus sign (+) indicates favorable growth. A minus sign (−) indicates an area in need of improvement.

1. SOCIAL AND EMOTIONAL DEVELOPMENT

a. ____ Gets along well with others
b. ____ Displays self-control
c. ____ Displays self-confidence
d. ____ Is willing to share
e. ____ Accepts suggestions and criticism

2. WORK HABITS

a. ____ Completes assignments
b. ____ Follows directions
c. ____ Works independently
d. ____ Has good attention span
e. ____ Is self-motivated
f. ____ Perseveres
g. ____ Is curious
h. ____ Displays resourcefulness
i. ____ Has pride in work
j. ____ Shows imagination

3. ACADEMIC AREAS

4. SUGGESTIONS TO PARENTS

5. PARENTS' COMMENTS

SPECIAL NOTE: This is a very serviceable form for you to keep. It allows for quick and accurate reference at all times.

Schedule

Teacher ______________________ Grade __________ Date ______________

TIME	MONDAY	TUESDAY	WEDNESDAY	THURSDAY	FRIDAY
1:30					
1:45					
2:00					
2:15					
2:30					
2:45					
3:00					
3:15					
3:30					
3:45					
4:00					
Evenings					
6:00					
6:15					
6:30					
6:45					
7:00					
7:15					
7:30					
7:45					

SPECIAL NOTE: Proper organization of time is a top priority with all teachers. This form allows you to do just that during those hectic conference times.

CUTTING

Referral Form

Teacher: ______________________________ Date: ____________

Please be informed that, on this date,

Student: ____

Grade: ____________________ Homeroom: __________________

was absent from my class,

Subject: ____________ Period: ____________ Room: ____________

although school records indicate that he/she was present on this date.

SPECIAL NOTE: It is always easier to fill out a form than to write an essay. The above form gives the chief disciplinary officer of your school all the information he or she needs in order to investigate further.

DISCIPLINE

Instant Disciplinary Referral Form

Student: ____

Date: ______________________ Time: ______________________

I am sending this student to the main office because he/she has committed a *serious disciplinary infraction.* I will complete a standard disciplinary referral form as soon as possible, but, in my professional judgment, this student had to be removed from the room *immediately.*

Teacher: ____________________

SPECIAL NOTE: If the incident had been serious enough to warrant referral to the office, then the situation is emotionally charged, and what you DON'T need is the misbehaving student hanging around while you fill out a school referral sheet. This form allows you to quickly remove the offender and gives you time to collect yourself before having to fill out the administrative paperwork.

EMERGENCY

Health Pass

School Year 19XX–19XX
EMERGENCY PASS

The student with this pass has my permission to report to the Health Office on an *emergency basis.* If there are any questions, please see me.

Teacher: ____________________________

SPECIAL NOTE: We usually cut a 4" x 6" piece of Masonite and print this message on it in indelible marker. Thereafter, should an emergency health or medical problem occur, this pass can be quickly given to the student.

EQUIPMENT

Location Form

This is a list of the educational equipment stored in this room for use with my classes. It is expected that all equipment will be returned to its proper location after use.

Teacher: ____________________
Room: ____________________

DESCRIPTION	SERIAL #	LOCATION

SPECIAL NOTE: This form not only serves as an inventory list for the equipment in your room, but, in the event of your absence, it is a handy reference guide for the substitute teacher or any other faculty member who may be using your room.

Request for Emergency Repair

Date: ____________________

To: ____________________
From: ____________________

Re: EMERGENCY REPAIRS

This is an *emergency situation.* An item of educational equipment, which is a vital part of my teaching strategy, has broken down. Specifically:

Item: ____________________
Problem: ____________________
____

Please let me know, *as soon as possible*, when I may send this item to you for repair.

I thank you for your prompt attention to this matter. The sooner this item can be repaired, the sooner our students will benefit from its use.

SPECIAL NOTE: It is a major frustration to have a piece of educational equipment sit useless as you are forced to go through the "paperwork" to have it repaired. Find out who is in charge of your A-V equipment and try this note the next time something breaks down. It gets results.

FIELD TRIP

Evaluation Form

Date of Trip: ______________________

Group Taken: ______________________

Teacher(s): ______________________

Nature of Trip: ______________________

Bus Carrier: ______________________

RATING	HIGH	4	3	2	LOW
Bus Service					
Student Interest					
Simplicity of Arrangements					
Treatment at Destination					

Would you take this trip again? ( ) YES ( ) NO

Why or why not? ______________________

____

____

Overall evaluation of trip: ______________________

____

____

____

SPECIAL NOTE: You are the only one to see this form. It is to be kept as part of your personal records for evaluating and planning all future field trips.

GIFTED STUDENTS

Project Evaluation Form

Name: ______________________________ Date: ____________

Project Title: ______________________________________

Date Approved: ______________ Date Completed: ____________

Number of weeks it took and why: ______________________

____

Where did you get the idea for this project? ____________

____

Did you plan well? Why or why not: ____________________

____

Did you enjoy this project? Is there more to learn about this subject? Do you think you will ever return to it? ______________________________

____

Did you encounter any problems in this project? What were they? How were they solved or did you solve them? ________________________

____

Did you accomplish your objective? Why or why not: ____________

____

Did you learn something new? About yourself? About others? ________

____

SPECIAL NOTE: This form can be used as a starting point for discussion and discovery with the gifted student. As you can see, the emphasis is on the personal growth of the child, with provision made for the student to learn as much by failing at something as by succeeding.

HALLS

All-Purpose Pass

Student: ______________________________ Date: ____________

Teacher: ______________________________ Time Out: ____________

DESTINATION

( ) Lavatory ( ) Health Office

( ) Room ____________ ( ) Library

( ) Main Office ( ) Guidance Office

( ) Stock Room ( ) Custodian

( ) Other: ____

____

SPECIAL NOTE: This is a time-saver. A quantity of these stored in your desk will save you hours of time in writing out long passes. If you have any special areas in your school to which a student may be sent, add them to the check-off list as well.

INSTRUCTION

Progress Report

Student's Name: ______________________ Grade: __________
Subject: ______________________ Date: __________
Status of student's progress as of above date:
____
____

Causitive Factors (in instructor's professional opinion):
____
____

Observed strengths:
____
____

Observed weaknesses:
____
____

Recommendations and comment:
____
____

Signature of teacher:
____

SPECIAL NOTE: This is not a form you would use to report to parents. Rather, on those occasions when you receive requests for academic evaluations of a student from the child study team or school psychologist, this form is easily filled out and contains all the necessary information.

JOURNAL

Form for Daily Entries

Teacher: ____________________ Date: __________

DAILY JOURNAL

Subject: ____________________ Room: __________

Remarks: ______________________________

____

____

Subject: ____________________ Room: __________

Remarks: ______________________________

____

____

SPECIAL NOTE: This could be as long as you needed, of course. It is meant to be kept in your planbook or some other convenient place, and in it, you would place those significant events that happened in the class on a particular day. These might include behavioral problems, requests from administration, special assignments, etc. Thereafter, it serves as a record of your actions.

KEYS

Distribution List for Lockers

Teacher: ______________________ Date: __________

Page __________ of __________ Homeroom: __________

KEY #	SERIAL #	LOCKER #	STUDENT

SPECIAL NOTE: This is the type of list that is invaluable when problems arise, as they invariably do, with student lockers. This will tell you at a glance all the information you will need concerning keys for lockers.

Distribution Sign-out Sheet

Teacher: ______________________________ Homeroom: ______________

KEY SIGN-OUT SHEET

Key # ______________ Serial # ______________ Date: ______________

Key opens: ____

Given to: ____

Purpose: ____

Signature (key out): ______________________________________

Signature (key in): ______________________________________

Confirmed (teacher): ______________________________________

Key # ______________ Serial # ______________ Date: ______________

Key opens: ____

Given to: ____

Purpose: ____

Signature (key out): ______________________________________

Signature (key in): ______________________________________

Confirmed (teacher): ______________________________________

SPECIAL NOTE: Many times teachers must give out keys for their rooms, stockrooms, stage doors, etc., for a variety of reasons. This form keeps track of what key was given out, to whom, and for what reason. The signing of the key in and out by the person receiving it and the confirmation of the teacher make this a legal record in the event that anything happens while the key is in someone else's hands.

LAVATORY

Use Record

Teacher: ______________________ Date: ______________________

Subject: ______________________ Room/Period: ______________________

STUDENT	TIME OUT	TIME BACK

SPECIAL NOTE: Let's face it; we all know that kids abuse lavatory passes, some making the lavatory into their private clubhouse. If you suspect something of this nature, try keeping the form above for a week or so and perhaps have other teachers try it for the same time period. When you compare sheets, you will be amazed to see the patterns emerge of those FEW students who practice lavatory abuse.

LEARNING

Referral Form

To: Learning Disabilities Specialist

Teacher: ______________________________ Date: ______________

Grade/Subject: ______________________ Homeroom: ____________

I have reason to believe that the following student may have a learning disability, and I hereby tender his/her name for evaluation.

Student: ____

Age: _______________________ Grade: _________________________

I believe this student may have a learning disability for the following reason(s):

____

____

____

____

I stand ready to help in any way possible.

Teacher: ____________________

SPECIAL NOTE: Before your LDS or LDTC can help a child with a learning disability, they must be made aware that the problem exists. You are in the best position to spot these difficulties while they are still at a stage where they can be helped. This form is short and to the point and asks for nothing more than an evaluation. It is a quick method of getting help. Send it directly to the LDS or LDTC.

LOCKERS

Classwide Locker Assignment Sheet

Teacher: ______________________________ Date: ______________

School Year: __________________________ Homeroom: ___________

LOCKER KEY #	LOCKER #	ASSIGNED TO:

SPECIAL NOTE: This is a simple list, but it allows you to tell at a glance who has what locker and to whom that key you found belongs. It's a timesaver.

MEETINGS

Form for Taking Minutes

Organization: ______________________________

Secretary : ______________________ Date: __________

Time Started: ______________ Time Ended: ______________

Minutes of Last Meeting: ( ) Approved ( ) Not Approved

Comment: ______________________________

____

Reports: ______________________________

____

Old Business: ______________________________

____

New Business: ______________________________

____

Motions, Discussions and Results: ______________________________

____

Resolutions: ______________________________

____

For Next Meeting: ______________________________

____

Other: ______________________________

____

Adjourned: ______________________________

____

Signature of Secretary: ______________________________

SPECIAL NOTE: This form is for use by a student secretary for help in taking the minutes of a class or school club meeting. Later, as the student learns more about parliamentary procedure and note-taking, this sheet may not be necessary, but it is a good way to teach the student and still make certain that all pertinent information is gathered.

MEMOS

Quick Checklist

To: ______________________

From: ______________________

Date: ______________________

( ) Please see me	( ) Let's discuss
( ) Please review	( ) Please advise
( ) For your approval	( ) Please initial and return
( ) Please circulate	( ) As you requested
( ) For your action	( ) For your information
( ) For your files	( ) May I have your opinion?

( ) Other (comment): ______________________

____

____

Signature: ______________________

SPECIAL NOTE: Have this run off and cut up into individual sheets and you have a great timesaver for those myriad times when you must send a magazine article to a colleague, a record to the office, or anything else that does not require a long explanation. This is easily filled out and clipped to whatever is being sent.

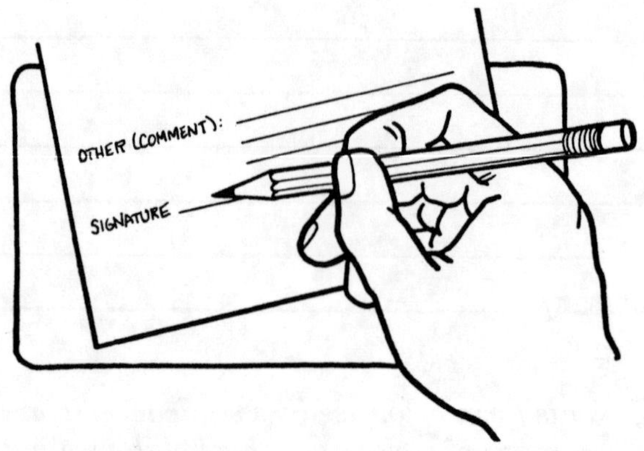

Short Message

To: ______________________________

From: ______________________________

Date: ______________________________

Re: ______________________________

____

Comment: ______________________________

____

____

____

------------------------------------Please Detach and Return------------------------------------

I have read your memo dated: ______________________________

Comment: ______________________________

____

____

Signature: ______________________________ Date: ______________

SPECIAL NOTE: This form is as easy to reproduce as the preceding one, but it gives you space to elaborate and even provides a space for a return message if so desired.

MONEY

Collection Form

Teacher: ______________________________

Money Collected For: ______________________________

STUDENT'S NAME	DATE IN	AMOUNT

SPECIAL NOTE: This is one of those "utility" forms that you can run off in bulk and use at various times during the year when monies must be collected. Staple it to the outside of a manila envelope, and you'll have everything in one place.

MONTHLY REPORT

Tutoring

Teacher: ______________________________ Date: ____________

Pupil being tutored: ______________________________

Grade: ____________ Homeroom: ____________

In what subject(s): ______________________________

Reason for tutoring: ______________________________

Report for the month of ____________, 19____

Dates when student was tutored: ______________________________

____

Time per session: ____________ Total time for month: ____________

Textbook(s) used: ______________________________

____

Pages covered in book(s): ______________________________

____

Progress of student: ______________________________

____

Problems: ______________________________

____

Comments: ______________________________

____

Signature of teacher: ______________________________

SPECIAL NOTE: If you are doing tutoring where the assignment has been given to you through the school, they will expect a report on that tutoring. If you are not supplied with a school form, you will find that this one supplies all the necessary information in a professional manner.

Teacher's Report Form

Teacher: ______________________________ Date: ______________

Subject(s): ____________________ Grade(s): ________________

Room(s): ____

Outstanding events or activities: ___________________________

____

____

Condition of room or school that requires attention: ____________

____

____

Student(s) requiring special services: ________________________

____

____

Special problems: _______________________________________

____

____

Comments: ____

____

____

Signature of teacher: _____________________________________

SPECIAL NOTE: If monthly reports are required of you, we feel that this form will cover all the essentials, and it won't take you forever to fill out, either. Naturally, you could add any additional categories your school may require.

NEWS

Information Sheet

Name: ______________________ Date: __________

Subject of story: ______________________

Who (those involved): ______________________

____

What: ______________________

____

When: ______________________

____

Where: ______________________

____

Why: ______________________

____

Other information: ______________________

____

SPECIAL NOTE: As you know, these are the five W's of a good news story. This form is very helpful in organizing any news story you must write, and it is invaluable for students working on a school or class newspaper.

PASS

All-Purpose

Name: ______________________________ Date: ____________

Please excuse the student named above. This student is to report to:

____

Date: ______________________ Time: ______________________

Teacher requesting student: ______________________________

Date of request: ______________________________

SPECIAL NOTE: While this is short, it is the type of utility instrument that is used very often throughout the year and saves a great deal of time and trouble.

Multi-Purpose

Date: ____

Time: ____

Student: ____

Reason for Excuse:

________ Main Office

________ Health Office

________ Library

________ Lavatory

________ Excused Tardiness by Teacher

________ Room # ____________

________ Other (Explain): __________________

____

Teacher: ______________________________ Room: ____________

SPECIAL NOTE: Here is another utility item. Often, the student can fill out all of the pass except for the teacher's signature, and the teacher can merely check it for accuracy before signing, thus saving a great deal of time.

PROFILE SHEET

Informational Sheet

Name: ______________________________

Teaching experience (positions, schools, dates): ______________________________

____

Educational background (institutions, degrees, dates): ______________________________

____

Work experience outside education: ______________________________

____

Extracurricular activities sponsored: ______________________________

____

Community-related service: ______________________________

____

Professional and recreational clubs and organizations: ______________________________

____

Awards, honors, publications: ______________________________

____

Areas of personal interest: ______________________________

____

Noteworthy characteristics: ______________________________

____

SPECIAL NOTE: When you have to write a résumé or fill out an application for an educational position, this is the form to use first. This will allow you to organize your strong points so you can present them to best advantage.

PUBLIC RELATIONS

Idea Submission Sheet

Name: ______________________________________ Date: ______________

I believe that the following would be a good subject for public relations releases for our school: ____

____

____

____

SPECIAL NOTE: Notice that the form is particularly short. In using this form, those teachers who have ideas can submit them to you, and you can evaluate them in a few seconds. This is certainly better than having to pour over sheets of writing. Then, when you spot a newsworthy idea, you can easily follow up with the particular teacher.

READING

Progress Report

Progress report of: ______________________ Grade: __________

Instructor: ______________________ Date: __________

Reading grade level on entering program: ______________________

Areas of improvement: ______________________

____

Areas where improvement is needed: ______________________

____

Recommendations for improvement: ______________________

____

Comments: ______________________

____

Signature of instructor: ______________________

SPECIAL NOTE: This report is of a nature that it could be sent to a parent or be used to supply information to a reading specialist of the Child Study Team. Notice that it includes both progress and improvements needed.

SELF-EVALUATION

Teacher's Form

The following is an aid for self-analysis. Place an X in each box that best describes you for that particular item.

ITEM	ALWAYS	USUALLY	SOMETIMES	SELDOM	NEVER
1. I possess competence and knowledge in my field of work and strive for continued professional improvement.					
2. I maintain physical capability, alertness, and emotional readiness to teach.					
3. I exhibit high standards of moral and ethical conduct, and employ a wholesome sense of humor in dealing with people.					
4. I am fair and impartial in the treatment of pupils and recognize the dignity of the child.					
5. I exhibit an understanding and acceptance of individual differences among students and provide for those differences.					
6. I communicate well with parents.					
7. I contribute significantly to the total functioning of the school.					
8. I explore and openly evaluate new approaches to teaching.					
9. I am receptive to suggestions for improvement.					

SPECIAL NOTE: We all need to look at ourselves from time to time and sort out our professional lives. This checklist, if done honestly, is an excellent step in that direction.

Student Interest Inventory

Name: ______________________ Birthdate: ______________ Age: _____

Do you have any brothers or sisters? If so, what are their names and ages? ___

____

Do you have a pet? If so, what kind? ______________________________

What would you like to do (occupation) when you get out of school? ______

What do you think your parents would like you to do when you get out of school?

____

Name the thing or things in which you are the most interested.

____

Do you read the newspaper? If so, what part(s)? ____________________

What's the best movie you have ever seen? _________________________

Name the sport you like best (or want to learn). ____________________

If we took a class trip, where would YOU like to go (number 1, 2, 3, etc.)?

( ) a museum
( ) a big city
( ) the planetarium
( ) the mountains
( ) a camping trip
( ) the beach
( ) a play in a theatre
( ) an amusement park
( ) other __________

Choose three of the following that you would like to do (number 1, 2, 3):

( ) do some art work
( ) listen to music
( ) see a movie
( ) play an instrument
( ) act in a play
( ) play a board game
( ) cook something
( ) take photographs
( ) read comic books

Put down the names of two famous people (they can be living or dead) about whom you would like to learn more:

____

Finish this statement: "If I could have only one wish, I'd wish for ________."

Do you like to read? If so, what kinds of books, magazines, etc., do you like? __

____

Finish this statement: "I think that teachers ______________________________

____."

SPECIAL NOTE: *Even granting that some children will give answers that they think you want or will like, there is still enough here for you to get a fairly good insight into your students. Anything that helps you understand the children you teach helps you be a better teacher. One word of caution: Don't include that final question unless you have a firm grip on your security blanket and your sense of humor!*

STUDENT INTERVIEW

Checklist

Student: ______________________ Date: __________
School year: ______________ Interview #: __________
Subject: ______________ Homeroom number: __________
____

Grades: ______________________________________
____

Attitude: _____________________________________
____

Behavior: _____________________________________
____

Special problems: ______________________________
____

Social and emotional growth: ______________________
____

Comments: ____________________________________
____

SPECIAL NOTE: This is a form for your benefit and becomes part of your private files. Just a few words of commentary in each section during or just after the interview can provide you with a great deal of insight into the student's progress, and it may even provide a tangible record of your attempts to help should that ever be needed.

STUDENT TEACHER

Evaluation Form

Student Teacher: ______________________________

Date: ______________ This is my ______________ evaluation.

Evaluation of overall progress to date: ______________________________

____

Areas in which improvement has been noted: ______________________________

____

Areas in which improvement is needed: ______________________________

____

Special areas of praise or concern: ______________________________

____

Comments: ______________________________

____

Signature of cooperating teacher: ______________________________

SPECIAL NOTE: The college will expect you to report on the student teacher sent you. Usually, the college has its own forms, but, if it does not, this form is sufficient for a general evaluation of progress.

Observation Form

Observation of ______________________________

Date ____________ Subject ____________ Period ____________

Number of students ____________ Time of day ____________

ITEM	GOOD	SATISFACTORY	NEEDS TO IMPROVE
Controls class			
Handles problems			
Has rapport with students			
Presents material/subject clearly			
Teaches facts			
Teaches concepts			
Provides for individual differences			
Uses time and materials to advantage			
Has a sense of humor			
Is creative			

Observer's comments: ______________________________

____

Student teacher's comments: ______________________________

____

This is the ____________ observation of this student teacher.

______________________________ ______________________________

Signature of observer Signature of student teacher

SPECIAL NOTE: This form was developed to help our student teachers and to impress upon them the seriousness of what they were doing. You can, of course, add any additional items to the form.

SUBSTITUTE TEACHER

Informational Sheet

Dear Substitute:

Thank you for covering my classes while I am absent. I hope you have a pleasant time. In order to help you, I have attached a copy of my regular schedule as well as work for three days, clearly labelled "Day One," "Day Two," and "Day Three." Please use them in that order.

Here is some other information you might need to know.

Location of:

a. seating charts ______________________________

b. plan book ______________________________

c. first-aid kit ______________________________

d. practice paper ______________________________

e. lavatory passes ______________________________

Fire drill procedure: ______________________________

____

Special problems: ______________________________

____

Special duty assignments: ______________________________

____

Dismissal procedure: ______________________________

____

Other interesting stuff: ______________________________

____

____

I have arranged for a colleague, ______________________________, in room ______, to look in from time to time during the day to see if you need anything. If you do, please do not hesitate to ask.

SUBSTITUTE TEACHER (Continued)

Enjoy the students, have a good day, and thanks again for substituting for me.

SPECIAL NOTE: This is the type of form that could be duplicated at the beginning of the school year and attached to those "emergency lesson plans" we all prepare for those times when we are unexpectedly absent. Of course, you could adapt this form to whatever information you deem necessary for your class(es). One side effect of this form is that word gets around among substitutes about how much you care, and substitutes often go out of their way to see to it that your plans are carried out precisely and the room is exactly as you left it.

Report to Teacher

Teacher: ______________________________
Substitute: ______________________________
Date(s) of coverage: from ______________ to ______________

CLASS	CLASSWORK COMPLETED
Period one	
Period two	
Period three	
Period four	
Period five	
Period six	
Period seven	

Special problems:

Disruptive students:

Comments:

Please leave this form, all work collected, and any other materials in the main office prior to leaving. Thank you.

SPECIAL NOTE: This is a general form that you might leave with your emergency lesson plans. It is easily filled out, gives the substitute a chance to tell you if anything significant has happened, and even lists disruptive students.

SUPPLIES

All-Purpose Requisition Form

Name: __________________________________ Date: ____________

Department: ___________________________ Homeroom: ____________

This is my _______ request of the 19____–19____ school year.

ITEM	CODE #	QUANTITY

Comments: ____

____

____

Signature: __________________________________ Date: ____________

SPECIAL NOTE: The advantage of this form is that it allows you to comment, perhaps about the necessity of the supplies being delivered quickly. Also, it shows that you have not "bugged" the supply officer with constant requests. For these points alone, it is likely to be fulfilled quickly.

TASKS

Description of Student Job Form

Student: ______________________________

From: ______________ To: ______________

AREA	TASK	TIME

Special duties: ______________________________

____

Special instructions: ______________________________

____

____

Teacher: ______________

Date: ______________

SPECIAL NOTE: All students get assigned tasks to do around the classroom as a matter of course. This form is valuable if you are trying to develop responsibility in a particular student, as everything is specifically spelled out.

Weekly Task Assignment Calendar

Teacher: ________________________ Room: __________

Job assignments for the week of ________________________

STUDENT	DATE AND TASK			

SPECIAL NOTE: This calendar makes life a lot easier around the classroom. For the first few weeks, however, you may have to prompt the students to check the bulletin board every day, but soon it becomes a matter of mere routine.

TEACHER'S AIDE

Report to Teacher

For the dates ____________________ to ______________, 19____

Students tutored and in what subjects: ________________________

____

Assignments completed: ________________________________

____

Total hours in classroom: ______________________________

____

Total hours other than classroom: ________________________

____

Total hours for period: ________________________________

____

Conditions that should be brought to attention of teacher: __________

____

Comments: ____

____

Signature of teacher's aide: ____________________________

Date: ____________________________

SPECIAL NOTE: You may wish to provide more space under various headings or add some headings of your own. It is a written record of what was accomplished by your aide and gives you formal notification of procedures as well as one basis for your aide's evaluation.

TELEPHONE

Conversation Report Form

Date of call: ______________________ Time of call: ______________

Caller: ______________________ Person called: ______________

Reason for call: ____

____

Summary of call: ____

____

____

Comment: ____

____

Signature of teacher: __________________________________

Date: __________________________________

SPECIAL NOTE: *This form would fit nicely on a 4" x 6" index card. Every time you call a parent or a parent calls you, it takes a moment to fill out this form. You would then have a written and legal record of all calls to and from you.*

TEXTBOOKS

Classwide Record Form

Teacher: ______________________ Homeroom: ____________

School year: 19____–19____ Subject: ______________________

Book title: ______________________________________

Publisher: ______________________________________

STUDENT	DATE ISSUED	CONDITION WHEN ISSUED	DATE RETURNED	CONDITION WHEN RETURNED	COMMENTS

SPECIAL NOTE: Again, this is the type of form that can be reproduced in quantity to serve you for a long time. Use one sheet per class per book, and you will always have a handy and quick reference source for use throughout the school year for returning lost books, telling if a book has been abused, etc.

Evaluation and Selection Form

EVALUATION FORM FOR TEXTBOOK SELECTION

Title: ______________________________

Publisher: ______________ Copyright date: ____________

New or revised edition: ________ Author, editor, etc.: ____________

Specific subject matter covered: ______________________________

____

Content evaluation:

Is subject matter correct in terms of present-day knowledge? ________

Does it provide the desired scope or sequence? ________

Is it appropriate for age level(s) intended? ________

Does it cover the skills/knowledge it proposes to impart? ________

Can it serve as resource material as well as a basic text? ________

Comment on the instructional strategies used: ______________________________

____

Comment on availability of materials (visual aids, workbooks, tapes, overhead projector materials, filmstrips, etc.) to be used in conjunction with textbook:

____

____

Evaluator's comments: ______________________________

____

____

Date: ____________ Signature of evaluator: ______________

SPECIAL NOTE: Serving on a committee to select new textbooks can often be a frustrating job. If you are in such a position, a form such as this, filled out by each member for each considered text, can be a great help when it comes time to make a final decision.

UTILITY

All-Purpose Form

Title:					
Responsibility:					
Objective:					
ACTIVITIES	STAFF	TIMELINES	RESOURCES	CONSTRAINTS	EVALUATION CRITERIA

SPECIAL NOTE: Whenever you are planning something on a large scale such as a committee project, this form is a tremendous timesaving and organizational tool. We suggest typing it up lengthwise in order to afford more room under each column. Then, you simply fill in what is required under each heading and you have, at a glance, all the necessary information for your entire project. This is also excellent for submitting a proposal to the administration, as all information is available on one sheet.

WORKSHOP

Evaluation Form

Workshop title: ______________________________

Date: ______________ Presenter(s): ______________________

According to your own understanding and in your own words, what was the primary concept developed during this workshop?

____

____

Were the objectives of the workshop met? If not, were any met? Which ones?

____

____

What aspect(s) of the workshop were most significant or important in helping to expound or develop the concept or meet the objectives?

____

____

Can you suggest ways in which this workshop might have been differently planned in order to contribute more effectively to the development of the concept?

____

____

What were the strongest and the weakest aspects of this workshop?

____

____

SPECIAL NOTE: How many workshops do you attend over a career in teaching? One hundred? More? How many of those do YOU give to others? If you are involved in either the planning or the giving of workshops, a form such as this, filled out by every participant, can help you evaluate what you are doing and improve your skills.

PART III

Handouts, Messages, and Informational Communications

Section 1

For Parents

CAREERS

Notice of Career-Day Program

Dear Parents:

On Thursday, March 22, at 1:00 P.M., we will be holding a special Career-Day program in our classroom.

Recently, your child and the other students of our class indicated several careers they might want to explore as possible choices for themselves in the future. We have been fortunate in obtaining several volunteers from our community who are currently engaged in those careers to come to our school to speak to our students concerning the educational requirements for the career as well as the rewards and responsibilities. The students are looking forward to it, and I am certain that it will be a rewarding and educational experience.

We would be delighted if you could join us on March 22. I am certain that you would find it as fascinating and illuminating as will I and the children.

Sincerely,

SPECIAL NOTE: If handled properly, Career Day can be a great deal of fun for everyone. The programs are also an excellent opportunity for establishing community goodwill because local newspapers will often accept a short article on the activity, particularly if you invite the mayor or a member of the city council. We have never had any difficulties getting volunteers to speak at these affairs.

CLASS EVENTS

Parental Interest Calendar

Dear Parents:

Another school year has begun. Over the years, I have come to appreciate the fact that most parents are very interested in those school activities in which their child is participating and to which parents are most cordially invited to attend. Indeed, problems have sometimes arisen when there has been lack of sufficient notice to allow scheduling on the part of busy parents.

Therefore, I have taken the liberty of drawing up the calendar of events for the coming school year to which you are herewith invited. I look forward to meeting you at them. Rest assured that if there is any change in time or plans, I will notify you well in advance.

SEPTEMBER—

24 —FALL FIELD DAY: Parents are invited to join their children for a day of games and athletic contests and exhibitions. 9:30 A.M.–2:15 P.M.

OCTOBER

15 —BACK-TO-SCHOOL NIGHT: Parents are invited to return to school, follow their child's daily schedule, meet the teachers, and hear what's happening in school. 7:30 P.M.–11:00 P.M.

28 —HALLOWEEN PARTY: A special party for Halloween; apple bobbing; "scary" stories; judging for best costume by class. 1:00 P.M.–2:30 P.M.

SPECIAL NOTE: Include not only those events peculiar to your class but also any school-wide activities such as those held for American Education Week. Send this form home as early in the school year as possible, and no one can ever say, "If only I had known..."

CONFERENCES

Notice of Date and Time

Dear Mr. and Mrs. ______________________:

From __________ to __________ on ____________, ____________ 19____, time has been set aside so we may confer together concerning your child's progress. The conference will be held in ______________'s homeroom.

For scheduled conferences to be successful, the time limits set must be respected. As the conference progresses, if we see that more time is necessary, we will arrange for an additional appointment.

Sincerely,

______________________, Teacher

------------------------------Please Detach and Return Promptly------------------------------

( ) We will attend the conference as scheduled.

( ) The time is inconvenient. I shall call the school and request another time.

Signature of Parent/Guardian: ______________________________

SPECIAL NOTE: Nowhere in this notice is it suggested that the parent might not want to come to the conference. Indeed, everything about it assumes the cooperation of the parent.

Questions Parents Should Ask

Before you come

- Ask if there is anything your child wants you to discuss with the teacher.
- Think about what you want to ask the teacher. Jot down your questions and bring them with you.
- Don't hesitate to bring information about your child's home life and attitude about school.

At the conference

- Relax! Your child's teacher and you want the same thing—a happy and successful child. You at home and the teacher in school are an ideal partnership to help the child.
- Don't be afraid to ask what the various report card terms mean. Many terms are new since you went to school and the teacher will be happy to explain them.
- Don't hesitate to take notes if you wish, especially if only one parent can attend the conference.

After the conference

- Discuss the conference with your child. Stress the positive strong points brought out by the teacher. Talk about suggestions for improvement and new goals.

Questions you may want to ask the teacher

- Do you think my child is working as well as he or she should be?
- What do you expect of me, as a parent with a child in your class?
- Does my child get along well with classmates? How about participation in group activities?
- What kind of discipline is used in your class? How does my child react to discipline?
- What books and materials is my child using in the classroom? In the library? Do you think they are appropriate for this grade level?
- Does my child always need direction from you or can he/she work alone?

Conferences are not just for parents and classroom teachers

The special-area teachers are in school, too, and would be happy to talk with you about your child. Make a note on your conference appointment sheet that you would like to see the art, gym, resource, supplemental teacher, or the

Questions Parents Should Ask (Continued)

librarian. The school will make every effort to see that they are available to meet with you when you are in that building.

Parents are welcome to come in to talk about their child's progress with a teacher or administrator at any time. Call the school secretary to ask for an appointment if an additional conference is desired.

SPECIAL NOTE: Quite often, parents are nervous and uncomfortable at conferences because they do not know what to ask or how to proceed. This type of handout gives parents questions to ask and outlines a good procedure.

FAILURE

Notice of Possible Student Failure

Dear ______________________________:

This is to inform you that your son/daughter, ____________________, grade ____, is doing unsatisfactory work in (subject) ________________, and may get a failing grade for the marking period that ends on ________________ unless something is done.

The purpose of this report is to bring this situation to your attention in order that the student, the teacher, and the parents, working together, may remedy the situation.

I have checked below some of the causes that seem to be contributing to your child's present difficulties:

( ) Absenteeism
( ) Poor Class Attitude
( ) Unsatisfactory Test Scores
( ) Major Behavioral Difficulties in Class or School
( ) Inattention in Class
( ) Work Not Done on Time
( ) Poorly Prepared Lessons
( ) Frequently Unprepared
( ) Little or No Homework
( ) Failure to Make Up Work
( ) Other: ____
____
____

Perhaps a conference might prove beneficial. If you feel that this would be the best course, please contact the school, and a convenient time will be arranged. Thank you for your cooperation.

Teacher: ________________________
Date: ________________________

SPECIAL NOTE: This is a form that may be used from year to year and takes very little time to fill out. It is always wise to send this about half way through the marking period so that there is adequate time to work with the failing student.

FOREIGN LANGUAGE

Invitation to Special Program

Dear Parents:

On Thursday, May 3, 19XX, at 8:00 P.M., the students in our various Foreign Language programs will be holding their annual Foreign Language Night presentation. This event will be held in the school cafeteria and involves students from the French, Spanish, German, and Russian classes of our school. They will be presenting sketches, songs, and authentic folk dances—all in the various foreign languages. For your refreshment, authentic dishes representing many foreign lands will be prepared and served by our students.

This event provides our students with the opportunity to practice the languages they have studied so hard to learn. It is also a very entertaining evening, and many parents have highly praised our students in past years. All we need for its complete success is our attendance.

We look forward to seeing you there.

Sincerely,

SPECIAL NOTE: This is the perfect note if you are the department coordinator or person in charge of such a program. You would, of course, suit it to your particular program, but this invitation gives all the particulars.

HOLIDAYS

Schedule for a Class Party

Dear Parents:

Once again, you have come through. I deeply appreciate your kindness in volunteering to help out during our Holiday Party. Following is a schedule of times and events. I hope this will prove helpful.

1:30—parents bringing refreshments arrive at school; check in with main office; come to room 207.

1:30–1:50—set up refreshments in room 207; the children will be at a special holiday assembly at this time; Mrs. Baker, teacher's aide, will be in the room to provide direction.

1:55—students return to room; parents help serve refreshments and supervise.

2:00–2:20—party time!

2:20–2:30—Special Holiday Program:
Arthur Roth—The Meaning of Channukah.
Maria O'Brien—What is Christmas?

2:30–2:50—games; please join in and help with the fun.

2:50–3:00—cleanup; children prepare for dismissal.

3:00—dismissal.

Thank you for helping. The children really look forward to this party, and I am certain that you will have just as much fun.

Sincerely,

SPECIAL NOTE: Whenever you have parental volunteers involved, and particularly for an affair of this type, it is always appreciated, and things go a lot more smoothly as well, if detailed information and scheduling can be arranged.

HOMEWORK

Guidelines

GUIDELINES FOR HOMEWORK

Homework can be a genuine extension of school learning when it provides opportunities to: recall, apply and review knowledge and skills; research new topics; work independently; develop responsibility and self-discipline; improve organization, study habits, and use of time; increase self-confidence. As with all opportunities for learning, homework can generate a positive attitude among students when it provides success. It should never be given as a punishment.

Homework is effective when: the purpose is clearly stated; it is an outcome of classroom instruction; assignments are varied and recognize individual differences; it is completed and evaluated; the tasks are challenging and meaningful; assignments are reasonable in length; parents view it as a constructive activity. Ideally, homework is effective when it comes from the students' own interests. Homework can occasionally be work not finished in class.

Students who leave class to participate in other programs, such as GATE or Basic Skills, are required to submit homework. At the teacher's discretion, assignments can be adapted to individual needs. Resource Room teachers will assign homework to their students.

LENGTH OF ASSIGNMENTS: Homework should be part of a regular routine, assigned four times a week, and rarely on weekends. Although there are no formal homework assignments in Kindergarten, it is expected that children and their parents will review each day's activities and papers together. In other grades, the approximate amount of time listed should be the maximum. Individual students vary in the pace with which they complete work; the times are average for each group.

grades 1 & 2	15 minutes
grade 3	30 minutes
grade 4	45 minutes
grade 5	60 minutes
grade 6	90 minutes
grades 7 & 8	120 minutes

SUGGESTIONS FOR STUDENTS:

- make sure you understand the assignment
- choose the same time and place to do your homework every day
- study where it is quiet — away from TV, radio, and conversation
- have all necessary materials ready before you start (books, paper, references, pen, and pencil)

- estimate the amount of time needed and pace yourself
- tackle the hardest subject first — save the best till last
- check your work for neatness and to correct errors
- take pride in your work and do your best
- don't leave home without it!

SUGGESTIONS FOR PARENTS:

- encourage your child to take pride in his or her work
- praise attempts to produce good quality work
- motivate the child who finds it difficult to concentrate on the task
- provide a well lighted, uncluttered environment that is quiet and without distractions of TV, radio, and telephone
- ask your child to explain the purpose of assignments, the directions, and what is expected
- be ready to help — direct, but don't do the homework
- check each day to see that assignments are completed
- look for ways to apply what your child is learning in school

SPECIAL NOTE: This is the type of informational handout that is very popular with parents, and it is a natural winner for such times as open house, back-to-school nights, and conferences. The good, solid advice given here can help establish a strong relationship between parents and teacher, which can only benefit the student.

IDEAS

Soliciting Ideas and Suggestions

Dear Parents:

Too often, people come up with great ideas that go nowhere. They think, "Nobody would be interested in this!" or "Why bother? Who'd listen?" How sad this is, because when people begin to think this way, their ideas die, and something that might have benefited many people is lost forever.

You are, after all, the people who know your children the best. Consequently, if you have any ideas about the functioning of the class or how to better reach them, I, for one, would like to hear about them.

Please share your ideas with me. I am certain that we can all profit from your knowledge, insight, and expertise.

Sincerely,

SPECIAL NOTE: While this is written in the form of a separate letter, there is no reason why it could not be included as part of your original greetings to parents at the start of the school year. It's a great way of building home/school rapport, but please don't send it unless you honestly want that byplay.

INTERVIEW

Request

Dear ____________________:

In order to discuss your progress for this marking period, I have arranged for an interview between us. This interview will be held on (date) __________ at (place) ____________________ at (time) ____________________

If this is inconvenient, please let me know at least one day previously.

____

Teacher's signature

SPECIAL NOTE: When we hold interviews with our students, we try to make it as formal as possible, in order that the student be impressed with the fact that this is a serious business that cannot be taken lightly. This formal notice helps to set the mood for the ensuing interview.

KINDERGARTEN

Preparing Parents

Dear Parents:

On _______________, _______________, 19____, your child will be starting kindergarten at our school. I hope that your child will find this a happy and enjoyable experience. I have taken the liberty of preparing this list of suggestions that have worked well in the past. I hope that they will prove helpful to you.

1. Come to school a little early and let your child explore the playground area. Show your child *exactly* where you will be waiting after school. Repeat this several times.
2. When I meet you and your child at the door to the school, please remain cheerful and happy, say goodbye, and leave quickly. It has been my experience that any tears on a child's part will disappear as the day's activities begin.
3. At dismissal time, please wait outside the building at the spot you pointed out to your child earlier. The children will be brought to you and released *only* to you. Indeed, if someone else is to pick up your child, you *must* notify the school.
4. Please remember that children are quick to pick up attitudes from adults. If you are enthusiastic, happy, and keep emphasizing how enjoyable school will be, your child will adopt these attitudes and have no trouble adjusting to school.
5. Kindergarten is a milestone in your child's life. Enjoy it together!

I look forward to meeting you and to working with you during the coming school year.

Sincerely,

SPECIAL NOTE: This is good, sound advice with which all kindergarten teachers can agree. The letter also provides direction to parents, which is greatly appreciated, particularly by parents who are going through this for the first time.

LEARNING

Notice of a Problem

Dear ______________________________:

We all like to hear good and encouraging news, and I think I have some for you. First, however, I must make you aware of a problem that your child seems to be having in class:

____

____

____

____

The good news is that I am certain that, working together, we can help your child overcome this problem and return to the level of academic achievement we know he or she is capable of.

Toward that end, I am making the following suggestions:

____

____

____

____

If you want to talk to me, of if I can help in any way, please contact me at the school.

Yours sincerely,

SPECIAL NOTE: This form could be used for anything from a student not handing in homework to one who is "goofing off" or "acting up" in class. It should NOT be used for the child with the actual learning disability, who must be handled by special means.

OPEN HOUSE

Guidelines for Those Attending

WELCOME TO OUR CLASSROOM!

We are very pleased you could visit with us. We hope you will enjoy your stay and will want to come again. Please take this opportunity to observe the various exhibits of student work located throughout the room and to sit in on a regular teaching session.

You will notice several folding chairs located in the rear of the room. Taking one of these seats will not only afford you observation of the entire class, but the students will be less distracted by your presence, and you will get an accurate picture of a classroom session.

Should you wish to tour the entire school, please ask in the main office, and a member of the Student Council will be happy to assist you.

This is your class. Enjoy your stay.

SPECIAL NOTE: Especially during American Education Week, parental visits to schools and classrooms are encouraged by the school. When this happens, it only makes sense for good class management; the students should be given some direction, albeit in a very positive manner, for their presence in your class. The form above could be handed out at the door to your room by a student assigned that chore, and your regular class time would be interrupted as little as possible.

PARENTS

How They Can Help

To guarantee the best possible education for a child, the home and the school must work together. Here are a few suggestions as to how this can be accomplished:

- Take an active interest in what is going on in the schools: attend school activities, come to Parent-Teacher Conferences, join the P.T.A., and attend Board of Education meetings.
- Encourage your child to talk about the school day. If you make it important to you, it becomes more important to your child.
- Notify the school of any changes in the home situation. Keep your work and emergency telephone numbers up to date.
- Contact the school about any school-related problem so someone can give it immediate attention.
- Review the homework guidelines with your child and follow the suggestions together. Keep the house quiet and free of distractions at homework time.
- Give your child realistic responsibility at home. Children learn competence by doing real work that helps the family.
- Show confidence in your child's ability to make decisions.
- Introduce your child to the world of work by discussing jobs that various people do and the service they provide.
- Remember to praise good work. Praise, when it is earned, is a great confidence builder.
- Resist the temptation to compare your child with other children, including brothers and sisters.
- Make sure your child gets plenty of rest and has an adequate diet. Encourage good health habits and allow free time for leisure activities.
- Be aware of the amount of television your child is watching. Try to keep a balance among outdoor activities, reading, hobbies, and television.
- Encourage interest in books, magazines, hobbies, trips, and current events.
- Have reading materials in your home. Discuss with your child your own interests and the books you are reading.

How They Can Help (Continued)

- Play games, especially those that have educational value, such as numbers games, guessing games, word games, some board games, chess, and dominoes.
- Help your child to notice details of the world around you. Point out changes in weather, seasons, and growing things. Visit interesting places and see new things that are different from what is seen at home or in school.

SPECIAL NOTE: ***This is an ideal handout for Back-to-School Night, Open House, or any other type of activity where parents will be visiting the school. Many parents appreciate having this good, sound advice.***

P.T.A.

General Flyer

The Rock Township Public Schools' Parent-Teacher Association (P.T.A.) works to help all children in the district. The P.T.A. fosters a close rapport between the schools and the home to encourage meaningful community involvement that will help our children to grow in every possible way.

The P.T.A. is involved in more than twenty projects during the year. Some of them are the Science Fair, class parents, Book Fairs, and school volunteers, the sale of school supplies, awards presented at graduation, and a graduation party. These are worthwhile projects that need parental help. Please volunteer your time, energy, and talent. Helping children can be a very rewarding experience.

The P.T.A.'s monthly newsletter is brought home by the students and will provide information about meetings and other P.T.A. activities. The P.T.A. Executive Council meets on the first Tuesday of every month at 8:00 P.M. in the All-Purpose Room of the Junior High School. All are welcome to attend these meetings.

If you are not already a P.T.A. member, we look forward to having you join with us to help our children.

SPECIAL NOTE: Quite often, teachers serve on P.T.A. committees. Should you find yourself in charge of getting out information, this is a highly appropriate message for a flyer to the students' parents.

SPECIAL EDUCATION

Request for Conference

Dear ______________________________:

It is always important for the home and school to work together for the benefit of the child, but in the field of special education it is particularly valuable to the child.

Therefore, it is our wish that parents be kept informed of their child's progress in our special education program. I have set up a meeting for this purpose:

Date: ______________________________ Time: ______________________________

Place: ____

If this is inconvenient for you, please call the school, and we will arrange a time that is convenient for everyone.

I look forward to meeting you.

Sincerely,

SPECIAL NOTE: It has been our experience that most parents, especially those with children in special education programs, are anxious to meet with the teacher and will come gladly at a time arranged for them.

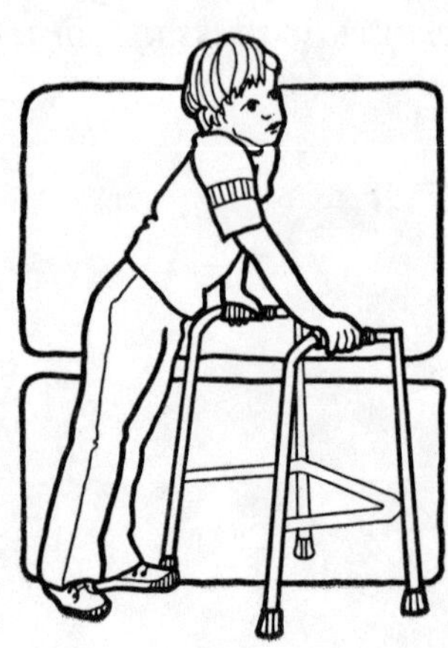

Notification of Special Program

SPECIAL PRESCHOOL PROGRAM FOR THREE- AND FOUR-YEAR-OLDS

The Mountainville School District is taking part in a statewide program to locate and provide services for any preschool child who may have a physical, mental, or emotional difficulty. The District feels strongly that children with handicaps deserve special attention and help as early in life as possible.

Some signs that a preschool child is having a problem and might need special attention are:

- trouble speaking or pronouncing words properly
- trouble walking or running
- difficulty manipulating small objects
- trouble seeing people or objects
- difficulty hearing voices or other sounds
- unusual quietness
- throwing frequent temper tantrums
- not getting along with others
- a particular health problem
- If you have or know of a child with any of these difficulties, please let us know. All children do not develop at the same rate, of course. We will arrange for a screening and, if a problem is confirmed, we will be able to advise the parent where help can be obtained.

Early detection means early help. Early help means, in many cases, that the problem can be partially or totally corrected before the child is old enough to enter kindergarten. This will lead the way for success in school, a chance that every boy and girl deserves.

Please contact the Special Services Office (123-4567) if you know of such a child in the Mountainville area.

SPECIAL NOTE: Whether it is this or a similar program, initial notification of parents is a must. Should you ever be in charge of establishing such a program, use this message with its information, conviction, and strong appeal as a model.

TUTORING

Request

Dear Parents:

Many parents have asked the procedures for obtaining a private tutor for their son or daughter, particularly in cases of a student's extended illness.

You must send such a request in writing to the Township Board of Education. Your request may be brought to this school, however, and it will be forwarded to the correct department. In your letter you must provide the complete name of your child, address, home telephone number, the school your child attends, the grade, and the subject or subjects in which you wish him or her to be tutored (for extended absence, simply say *all* subjects). Moreover, you must give a reason for your request, and, in cases of extended absence, the approximate length of the absence.

If the reason for the request is the extended illness and subsequent absence of your child, in almost all cases, a tutor will be provided by the district free of charge to you. If you request a tutor in order to gain additional instruction for your child, there will be a charge to you, and you will be notified of the specific charge before a tutor is assigned to work with your child. Children with extended illnesses are given priority in finding a tutor for them.

I hope that this information is of service to you. If I may help in any way, please feel free to contact me.

Sincerely,

SPECIAL NOTE: Of course, the exact procedures for requesting a tutor may vary from district to district, so you will describe YOUR procedures. Parents, however, are usually grateful for this information because many of them simply do not know how to go about it.

Report to Parents

DATE: ______________________________

Dear ______________________________:

This is a report on the progress of your child, ____________________, whom I tutored for the period from ____________________ to ____________________.

In that time, I tutored ____________________ in the following subject(s):
____
____

I used the following materials, books, etc.: ______________________________
____

The following is my professional opinion about your child's progress: ______
____
____
____

Sincerely,
Signature of Teacher: ______________________

SPECIAL NOTE: This is a simple form which is nonetheless effective for reporting the progress of a child you are tutoring. It is to the point, includes all necessary information, and keeps the parents abreast of their child's progress.

Section 2
For Students

ADULT STUDENTS

Welcome Message

WELCOME TO OUR CLASS!

All of life is an education. As someone who is an active part of our society, you are well aware that learning is not confined to the classroom; it is an ongoing process in which we engage every day of our lives. Indeed, the person who stops growing mentally soon finds that the world has passed him or her by. The person who continues to learn and seek out new knowledge finds life challenging and rewarding, and stays young at heart.

This is why I deeply respect your decision to continue learning as an adult. During this class, I hope to lead you into some new avenues of discovery, but, and I wish to make this very clear, I will need your help. As the class develops, I look forward to hearing *your* opinions, discussing *your* viewpoints, and sharing in *your* knowledge. I will learn as much from you as you from me.

SPECIAL NOTE: We usually distribute this message on the first night of class so that the adult learners can read it as we do the attendance-taking paperwork. The note goes a long way toward establishing rapport.

ASSEMBLIES

Zone Assignments

TO ALL STUDENTS:

Throughout the year we will be going from this room to the auditorium for a number of assemblies. Going to these assemblies will be as easy as 1, 2, 3, if we remember the following procedures. I have broken it down into four zones, and all you have to do is to remember what *you* have to do in each zone.

ZONE ONE	Wall of classroom along bulletin board	Line up quietly and wait until I or the person in charge gives the word to proceed. The last person out of the room closes the door.
ZONE TWO	Head of the south staircase	Proceed down the hallway to the head of the stairs. Wait there until given permission to continue.
ZONE THREE	Main hallway just inside main entrance	Proceed down the stairs. Turn right at the bottom and assemble in the main hallway, just inside the main entrance, and wait until given permission to continue.
ZONE FOUR	Doorway #6 to auditorium	Proceed down the hallway to entrance #6 to the auditorium. Wait in line until someone tells you where to enter and sit during the assembly.

When *returning* from assemblies, these zones are *reversed.* If we all cooperate, we should have a safe and enjoyable time going to, seeing, and returning from our assemblies.

SPECIAL NOTE: This procedure will work well if it is rehearsed several times. With everyone knowing where he or she belongs and what to do once there, everything should go smoothly.

CAREERS

Student Suggestions for Career Exploration

Name: ______________________________ Date: __________

Directions: We are planning to hold a Career Day for our class. We will invite people in many jobs and professions to come to school to tell us about their careers. In the space below, please tell me your choices for the careers YOU would like to hear about and *briefly* tell me why you are interested in those careers.

First choice: ______________________________

Why interested: ______________________________

____

____

Second choice: ______________________________

Why interested: ______________________________

____

____

Third choice: ______________________________

Why interested: ______________________________

____

____

SPECIAL NOTE: It has been our experience that children ALWAYS behave better and are more attentive in an activity in which they had a hand in planning. Three choices are allowed in this form because it may not always be possible to find someone who is a child's first choice, but it is almost always possible to find at least one out of the three.

CHANNUKAH/CHRISTMAS

Combined Message

This is the Holiday Season. At this time of year, we celebrate two great festivals: Christmas, which has been called a Festival of Love, and Channukah, which is known as the Festival of Lights. With love in our hearts, the world is always filled with light, and with light in our lives, there are no dark corners to fear.

Whichever holiday you celebrate, may I wish you LIGHT and LOVE throughout the coming year.

SPECIAL NOTE: Naturally, as teachers, we make every effort to accommodate ALL the religious beliefs of our students. This is a heartfelt message that would reach every child in your classroom.

CLASS NEWSLETTER

Sample Page

THE "211" EXPRESS

Vol. V, No. 3 December, 19XX

AN "APPLE" FOR THE CLASSROOM

On Thursday, December 1, 19XX, an Apple II computer was installed in our classroom. It is located at a work table in the back of the room, and many students have had a chance to use it.

So far, we have played some of the word games that came with it, but soon we are going to learn how it works and learn how to write "programs," which are the directions to the computer that tell it what to do.

The whole class is excited about this, and we are looking forward to learning about it.

Mary Beth Rielly

DECEMBER BIRTHDAY STARS
Billy Jenkins—7th
Lilly Sanders—10th
Harvey Brock—17th

WINTER HOLIDAY
December 19–January 2
HAVE FUN!!!

SPECIAL NOTE: This is the type of newsletter that a class might put together on a once-a-month basis. It could contain student-written articles about what the class is doing, interviews, a teacher message, and features about the children in the class. We have found that the kids and their parents love something like this. It is also a great public relations vehicle.

DISMISSAL

Rules

The following are the rules for *all* student dismissals, whether from the classroom or from a special activity such as an assembly program.

1. *Wait for permission:* Do not leave until given permission by the teacher or person in charge. The bell does not dismiss you, your teacher does.
2. *Listen to directions:* It is your responsibility to pay attention to special dismissal instructions. "I didn't know" is *not* an acceptable excuse.
3. *Proceed calmly:* Running, pushing, shoving, and fighting are not allowed.
4. *Be courteous:* Help your classmates. Be kind to others, and they will be kind to you.
5. *Know who's in charge:* If you have any special problems, go to the teacher in charge at once.

SPECIAL NOTE: It is always good to spell out rules of behavior in positive terms. It is also a good idea to send home all written rules so parents will know exactly what is expected of their child in school.

EXAMS

Hints and Procedures

Mid-term exams are upon us. If you have studied and worked all along, you should not be overly concerned. Here are some hints for preparing for and taking the exam:

1. On the afternoon and evening before the test, review your notes several times. Try to *understand* the material. Get a feeling for the body of the material instead of concentrating on memorizing details.
2. Get a good night's sleep and eat a good breakfast on the day of the test.
3. When you receive the test, read all questions before you write anything.
4. Answer those questions first with which you are most familiar; then go back to the others.
5. On multiple choice questions, eliminate those answers that are obviously wrong, then go with your first "educated guess" from those remaining.
6. If time remains when you have finished, reread your answers and make certain that you have said exactly what you wanted to say.

Remember, the important thing is to relax. If you have kept up with the work all along, you should do well.

SPECIAL NOTE: These suggestions are meant to be given to your students, so we have not gone into the very sound psychological reasons behind each.

Notice

TO: All my students
FROM: Mr. Hadley
RE: Final exams

Very soon you will be taking your final subject area examinations for the current school year. You have been given a schedule of the times and places for these exams, and I have posted a master list on our bulletin board as well.

Although I wish you success, I would like to remind you that if you have kept up with your studies all year long, you really have no need for "luck" and have nothing to worry about. By all means, study and review your notes, but remember that what you have learned over this past year has become a part of you, a part which you will be able to represent very well on a final examination.

Again, I wish you every success.

SPECIAL NOTE: This is the type of confidence-building "pep" note we like to give to students. It contains a basic truth and has a good influence upon the students, particularly the better students who, we have found, are the ones who tend to worry the most about exams.

EXTRACURRICULAR ACTIVITIES

Soliciting Student Membership

Now. . . you can

- Make friends
- Be a leader
- Have fun
- Learn valuable information
- Make a fortune (maybe)
- Get enjoyment that will last a lifetime

We can show you how!!!
It's easy!!! *It's fun*!!! *It's yours*!!!

The Thornton Junior High School
STAMP & COIN CLUB

2:30 P.M. Thursday, October 1, 19xx Room 203

WE NEED YOU!
BE THERE!

SPECIAL NOTE: While this may seem a bit overdone, we have seen it have a great effect upon students. This is particularly useful if you wish to swell the ranks of a club or activity to which you are the faculty advisor. Try it!

FIRE DRILLS

Zone Assignment Form

IN THE EVENT OF A FIRE DRILL

ZONE	LOCATION	TASK	STUDENTS
1	windows	close windows; pull blinds	
2	teacher's desk—center drawer	take plan book, mark book, and attendance book	
3	back of room	turn off sink; unplug all outlets	
4	classroom entrance	turn off lights and shut door	

SPECIAL NOTE: The blanks would be filled in with the names of students from the room with more than one assigned to each task in case one should be absent. A few drills, and each student should know exactly what to do in his or her zone in the case of an emergency.

GRADUATION

Message to Students

CONGRATULATIONS!

In a few days you will be graduating and will become an alumnus of this school. I know how excited and pleased you must be, and you have every right to be so—you have worked and studied, and now that final day is at hand.

I have heard many of you express your relief that soon you will be free of the school routine and can put aside the books and the papers and the projects and the reports. Perhaps this is as it should be, for after every great effort, there is the need for rest.

However, I would like to share a secret with you. It's a secret that many people don't discover until they are many years out of high school, and that some people never realize at all. That secret is simply that you are *not* finished with school at all; that everything you have gone through for the past twelve years has been nothing more than a preparation for the hardest and toughest school of all—life.

If a school is a place where you learn and grow, then life is, indeed, the final school in which we all learn. Day after day as you pursue your individual lives, you will be learning and growing. Indeed, the active mind never stops learning, never stops growing. The rewards will no longer be marks on a report card, but you will have to work for them just as hard.

I have come to know you and respect you. I know you have gotten an excellent preparation for the school of life, and I have every confidence that your achievements will be brilliant and your "marks" superb.

May good fortune and happiness follow you throughout your lives.

Sincerely,

SPECIAL NOTE: Perhaps some would call this overly sentimental and others might call it blatant propaganda, but there is not a single untruth in this letter. Indeed, this is precisely the type of thing, given to each student in a particular teacher's class, that is kept and remembered for years.

MONEY

Notice

TO: All my students
FROM: Mrs. Richardson
RE: Bringing money to school

We all need money at times in school to buy milk, lunch, a pencil, or a notebook. Some students, however, bring much more money to school than needed. This can lead to trouble.

There are people who would take that money from you, even if they had to hurt you to get it. In fact, we had some trouble just last week when one of our students was robbed of ten dollars on his way to school. Fortunately, he was not hurt, but his money is gone forever.

If the people who steal from others know that you do not carry a great deal of money, they would have little reason to risk stopping you. It would be a good idea, therefore, to only carry as much money to school as you need for that day. In that way, there need be no risk of theft.

Please have your parents sign this note and return it to me.

I HAVE READ THE ABOVE MESSAGE.

________________________________ ____________
Signature of parent/guardian Date

SPECIAL NOTE: We all know that outsiders, and even students within our own school, can prey on smaller children who carry large amounts of money. This message informs the children of that danger in clear and simple language, and allows the parents to share in your concern.

OPENING PROCEDURES

For a Class

TO ALL STUDENTS:

The opening procedures for each class shall be:

1. Bell rings—students come to order, take out homework, place it in upper right-hand corner of desk. Students take out textbook and turn to page displayed by teacher on blackboard.
2. Student Aide—during the above procedure, the student aide takes attendance in the teacher's attendance book, logs the name of absentees and tardies, and places these materials on teacher's desk.
3. Homework Monitor—collects homework, places papers on teacher's desk, lists students without homework, and places this list on teacher's desk.

If everyone cooperates, there is no reason why the class should not be able to begin an academic lesson within two minutes of the beginning bell.

SPECIAL NOTE: You would, of course, place in those procedures that you wanted followed in your classroom, but the form above will give you an idea. If these opening procedures are enforced, it will establish a good routine, and the class can get down to business with a minimum of distraction.

QUALITY

Message Concerning Assignments

TO ALL STUDENTS:

Throughout the school year, we will have quite a number of assignments, both homework and projects. While doing these assignments is important, the *quality* of your work is of equal value.

Homework and projects done carelessly show me that all you want to do is to get through the work as quickly as possible; that while you may have done the assignment, you may not have learned anything from it.

On the other hand, assignments that are neat, as free of errors as possible, and which go that extra step to show originality of thought and execution show me that you are taking pride in the *quality* of your work, and are probably learning a great deal from what you do.

So, by all means, do the assignments, but make a resolution now, and keep it all year long, to do the *very best* you can to keep your homework and projects of the highest quality you are capable of producing.

In that way, we will all be winners.

Your teacher,

SPECIAL NOTE: Any teacher who has corrected an assignment smeared with sticky substances of unknown origin can sympathize with this plea for quality homework. If you let your students know your wishes, and you enforce them for awhile, the students will soon be handing in quality work.

RULES

For the Bus

BUS RULES

1. Keep out of the streets. Use walkways.
2. Cross only at designated crosswalks.
3. Look before alighting from the bus and then go directly to the curb.
4. Never disturb the driver of the bus. Always remain in your seat.
5. When getting on or off the bus, do not crowd or push. Be courteous and follow the directions given by patrols.
6. Do not eat on the bus.
7. When riding in the bus, keep your head and arms within the bus.
8. Do not throw anything off the bus.
9. All patrols have been assigned for your safety. Therefore, follow their directions.
10. Constant bus offenders will run the risk of losing bus privileges.
11. The bus driver is the supervising adult on the bus. Obey the directions given by him/her.

SPECIAL NOTE: These rules are sensible and would make a good handout to students if you are the director of a safety patrol. Or, you might just want to distribute the rules to students prior to a class trip requiring the use of buses.

For a Classroom

CLASSROOM RULES

1. You are to be on time for class or have a pass explaining your tardiness. Unexcused tardiness is not permitted.
2. Always be polite. Extend courtesy and aid to those around you.
3. If you wish something, raise your hand and wait until you are recognized by your teacher. Then ask fully and completely.
4. Homework is due on the assigned day. Late homework will be penalized if there is no acceptable reason for its tardiness.
5. The bell does not dismiss the class—your teacher does.
6. Whenever there is a guest in the room, whether another teacher or another student, that guest is to be treated with respect.
7. You are here to learn. If you do not understand something, ask.
8. It is your responsibility to make up work after an absence. The same goes for missed tests and assignments. It is your responsibility to ask your teacher.
9. Extra help will be available to anyone who wants it. See your teacher and a convenient time will be arranged.
10. You are not likely to be allowed to throw things around or generally "mess up" your home. It is expected that you will take pride in your school as well. Before leaving the room, each student is responsible for cleaning the area around his or her desk.
11. The class will proceed in an orderly fashion. Consequently, there will be relative quiet unless otherwise instructed. If you want to speak, raise your hand and you will be recognized by your teacher.
12. If you need to use the lavatory or see the nurse, come to your teacher's desk and ask quietly.
13. Obscene, profane or vulgar language, hitting anyone, mocking anyone, destroying property, cheating, and bad manners *will not be tolerated at any time.*
14. All rules of the school apply to the classroom.

SPECIAL NOTE: These are good, solid rules for a classroom. Any rules, however, are only as good as the ways in which they are enforced. Post your rules prominently, so they may be referred to throughout the year.

For the Lunch Room and Playground

LUNCH ROOM/PLAYGROUND RULES

1. Students are to remain seated while having lunch.
2. Food or any other object is *not* to be thrown in the room.
3. Students are responsible for cleaning up after themselves after their lunch.
4. Students *should not* throw away their lunches.
5. Students are to have the permission of the teacher or supervising adult before leaving the lunch room for the playground.
6. Playground equipment is for the use of all students with the exception of those who misuse the equipment.
7. There are to be *no* tackle games played on the playground.
8. Students are *not* to bring in toys, games, radios, etc., to be used in school without the permission of their teacher.
9. Students *should not* enter the building (from playground) without permission of the teacher or supervising adult.

SPECIAL NOTE: Many teachers are assigned lunch or playground supervision as part of their duties. If you find yourself in charge of such activities, these rules are practical and, if enforced, keep the activity from getting out of hand.

STUDENT JOURNAL

Directions

TO ALL STUDENTS:

As I have told you, you are required to keep a journal in this class. The purpose of this journal is to get you used to writing and to putting your ideas on paper. You may keep your journal in whatever type of book you wish, but it must be a bound book (like a composition pad) where the pages will not fall out. If you do not have such a book, I will provide you with a duo-tang folder and punched paper.

You will be given ten minutes of class time each day in order to write in your journal. You may write whatever you wish, but I remind you that I will be collecting and reading these journals from time to time. I promise you that I will keep them confidential, but you should be aware that I will be reading them.

Later on, you will be using your journals as the basis of several writing assignments, so do a good job.

Put in your ideas, feelings, and observations. Enjoy it.

SPECIAL NOTE: The use of the journal in the teaching of writing is gaining more and more favor. Remind the student that you will be looking at what is written, so no student can ever claim that he or she was unaware of what was expected.

TELEPHONE

Usage Guide

TO ALL STUDENTS:

As you are aware, this school has two public telephones located just outside of the main office. These are for your use before and after school, during lunch period, during the passing of classes (provided you are not late for class), and in cases of emergency when you must contact home.

Therefore, I will not accept as an excuse for tardiness to class the fact that you were using the telephone. Nor will I permit you to leave class to use the telephone except in the case of an emergency. This "emergency" classification would be rare, indeed, and I reserve the right to determine what is and is not an "emergency" call. Calling home to find out if the letter arrived from your boyfriend or girlfriend, for example, is hardly an emergency, although I realize that it may seem quite important to you.

Let's be sensible and use the telephone in a realistic manner.

SPECIAL NOTE: Here, with a sense of humor and understanding, are some sensible rules that will help you avoid being deluged by requests to use the telephone.

USE

Message Concerning Facilities

TO ALL STUDENTS:

Now that the school year has begun, you are involved in your job—getting an education. As with any job, you also have available to you certain "tools of the trade."

Now, if a carpenter was going to build a chest, and he had all the wood and nails he needed, but refused to use a hammer or saw, what would you think of that carpenter? Not very much, I would guess.

So, too, you have all your tools available to you—the library, the textbooks, the study guides, and even me, your teacher. What would you think of yourself if you didn't use those tools to do your job? The teachers and staff of this school exist "to be used" to help *you* get a quality education.

Do not let your job—getting an education—go undone simply because you refuse to use the tools that are provided for you.

SPECIAL NOTE: Sometimes it feels as if our students expect learning to come through osmosis. A student must use what is available in order to learn. This is a message, given as early in the school year as possible, to reinforce that thought.

Section 3

For Teachers

AWARDS

News Release

FOR IMMEDIATE RELEASE:

Four seniors at Rock Township High School have been awarded college scholarships, which will be presented at graduation ceremonies to be held later this month at the school.

Walter Johnson and Maria Costanza will each receive a $1500 scholarship from the James Lucas Memorial Scholarship Fund. A scholarship in the amount of $5000 from the McGrath Corporation will be awarded to Thomas Belnath. A scholarship for full tuition from Michael's University will be presented to Sarah Roth, who will also receive Rock Township High School's Outstanding Citizenship Award.

According to school principal, John Benson, these scholarships are awarded on the basis of educational achievement, citizenship, and personal merit. "We are very proud of these outstanding students, and we are certain that they will continue to meet with success in college," he said.

The award ceremonies will be held as part of graduation proceedings to be held in the school auditorium on Thursday evening, June 23, at 7:30 P.M.

SPECIAL NOTE: Quite often, a teacher may be asked to compose a news release, especially if that teacher has been acting as class advisor or the like. Try to write all news releases with the most important facts in the beginning of the release. This is known as the "inverted pyramid" style and allows a newspaper to cut part of a story for reasons of space and still maintain the pertinent facts.

DETENTION

Notification Form

Student: ______________________________ Date: ______________

has been assigned detention by me on __________, 19_____ in Room ______ from __________ until __________.

The reason for this detention is: ______________________________

____

____

____

Signature of Teacher: ______________________________

SPECIAL NOTE: *This is a useful form which may be filled in quickly. It lends a note of serious authority to the occasion, and no student can ever claim that he or she wasn't sure or misunderstood. A copy of it may also be kept for your records.*

LUNCH

Daily Tally Sheet

DAILY LUNCH TALLY SHEET

Date: ______________________

Teacher: ____________________ Grade: _______ Room: _______

Lunch count: A: ___________ B: ___________ C: ___________

Teacher lunch: _______________ Teacher milk: _______________

Pupil milk: Chocolate: _______ Skimmed: _______ White: _______

SPECIAL NOTE: Particularly in schools without a central cafeteria, where students either eat lunch in the classroom or are brought to a sort of "all-purpose" room, accurate record-keeping is essential. A simple form such as this can go a long way toward making your paperwork easier.

NEWS

Guidelines

Do you have a newsworthy story?

Below are some guidelines for newsworthiness. Be honest and check the appropriate column for each with your story in mind. If you can check "yes" for seven or more, it is probably newsworthy. If not, then perhaps you might like to rethink it.

YES	NO	
( )	( )	Does your story concern something that goes beyond the day-to-day operation of the school?
( )	( )	Does your story emphasize positive interaction of students and faculty, or students and the community?
( )	( )	Does your story emphasize positive aspects of school life?
( )	( )	Does your story contain any unusual aspects that take it out of the realm of the mundane?
( )	( )	Would anyone besides the parents of the students involved need or want to know about the story?
( )	( )	Does the story have any humorous or heartwarming qualities?
( )	( )	Have all the facts of the story been checked for accuracy?
( )	( )	Does your story contain aspects with which a significant number of the general public could identify?
( )	( )	Could you provide black-and-white photographs if necessary?

SPECIAL NOTE: This checklist was originally put out by a school system's public relations office specifically as a guide to teachers about newsworthy stories. As you can see, it is tailored to the school and classroom, and it is a good guide if you are thinking of writing a news story about something in your class.

Sample News Story

A group of students at Rock Township High School have been roaming the halls interrupting classes lately, and the faculty and administrators are delighted.

It began in the Social Studies class of teacher Mary Norris. "We were discussing the plight of the people in Costa Grande, who had been devastated by a hurricane followed by the eruption of a volcano," Mrs. Norris reported. "My class was shocked and moved by the suffering of these unfortunate people."

"We felt we had to do something," recalls Tom Barron, a member of the class, "but we had no idea of how to go about it."

Mrs. Norris arranged for a visit by Mr. Frank Callerton, Associate Director of the American Relief Society. "I spoke to them of the urgent need for food, clothing, and medical supplies," stated Mr. Callerton, "and these wonderful kids did the rest."

After that, Mrs. Norris and her class went into action. During each class period for the next week, students visited other classes in the school, informing them of the desperate need of Costa Grande residents and asking for donations of food and clothing.

"They were marvelous," Mrs. Norris remembers. "The entire school reacted so well that we had a real problem of where to store the materials that were coming in."

"In all," reports Rock Township High School principal John Benson, "our students raised an estimated seven thousand dollars' worth of supplies. We are proud of them and their actions, which bespeak the fine character of our students and the community."

The accumulated materials will be accepted by the American Relief Society at a school-wide assembly to be held next Monday morning at 10:00 A.M. at the school.

SPECIAL NOTE: This is a type of "feature" article that newspapers will take for publication. Notice how the opening paragraph catches the reader's attention and makes him or her want to read on. Notice, also, that all pertinent information is included.

Soliciting Information for a Newsletter

TO ALL STUDENTS:

The next issue of our class newsletter, "The '211' Express," will be published on ______________________________.
We need your ideas and your help. Please fill out this sheet and return it to me.

Thank you,
Mrs. Porter

I think a good idea for the newsletter would be: ____________________
____

I volunteer to: ______________________________
____

Signed: ______________
Date: ______________

SPECIAL NOTE: This allows the students a say in what shall be included in the newsletter, but it does not allow them to merely make a suggestion and then sit back. Rather, it calls for active participation in the doing as well as the planning.

Soliciting News Coverage

Dear News Editor:

As a subscriber and reader of your newspaper, I am very much aware of the high quality of news coverage your paper represents. I am also aware that you make a continuing effort to provide extensive coverage of newsworthy local events.

I believe that there is just such an event about to occur that would merit the attention of your news staff.

On Saturday morning, April 30, 19XX, on the grounds of Thornton Junior High School, a special "carnival day" will be held. While this in itself is not a unique occurrence, the story behind it is one that is extremely rewarding.

When one of our students suffered a tragic accident that left him a paraplegic, our students went to work for that boy and his family. Through a great deal of hard work and dedication, our students have raised over $9,000 for their friend and classmate. This carnival will be the culminating event in that effort.

All of the students who have worked so long and hard will be present as will the young man and his family. State Senator Norman Kauth, who has taken a special interest in this case, will also be there to present a final check to the family.

I sincerely feel that this event is worthy of coverage by your newspaper. If I may provide any further information or be of any further service, please do not hesitate to call on me.

Sincerely,

SPECIAL NOTE: In asking for news coverage, your best bet is to contact your local newspapers first. Quite often, they will arrange to have an event covered and even a photographer assigned to it if they can be convinced that it is newsworthy. The presence of some well-known person or a political figure almost assures coverage.

OBSERVATION

Anecdotal Record of Student Observation

Observation of Jennifer Brady on Thursday, May 22, 19XX from 11:00 A.M. to 11:30 P.M. in Room 110.

Jennifer is seated at her desk. She takes a pencil from behind her ear and begins to draw or write on the surface of her desk.

The teacher announces a math quiz and starts to pass out paper. Jennifer receives the paper from the child in front of her. She takes a sheet and tosses the remainder over her head without looking. The paper scatters. Jennifer laughs. The teacher asks Jennifer to pick up the paper. Jennifer says nothing. As the teacher turns toward the blackboard, Jennifer extends the middle finger of her right hand in the teacher's direction. She picks up the paper and slams it on the desk of the student behind her. She sits down and punches the student in front of her.

The quiz begins, and Jennifer stares out the window. She writes nothing. After the second question, she puts her head in her arms folded on the desk. She remains in this position for the remainder of the time.

SPECIAL NOTE: Often, teachers are asked to compile anecdotal records on children being evaluated by the Child Study Team or other school agencies. Always remember to keep these records OBJECTIVE, reporting ONLY what was observed. Don't say, for instance, that Jennifer insulted the teacher. Rather, just describe the action you observed.

Observation of Social Interaction

Student: ______________________________ Date: ______________

Class: ______________________ Time: from __________ to __________

Number of contacts with teacher: ______________________________

A. Contacts initiated by teacher: ______________________________

B. Contacts initiated by subject: ______________________________

Number of contacts with other students: ______________________________

A. Contacts initiated by other students: ______________________________

B. Contacts initiated by subject: ______________________________

With whom were most contacts made: ______________________________

A. How many contacts: ______________________________

B. How many initiated by student: ______________________________

C. How many initiated by subject: ______________________________

Names of students surrounding subject's desk:

A. ____________________ E. ____________________
B. ____________________ F. ____________________
C. ____________________ G. ____________________
D. ____________________ H. ____________________

Nature of subject-initiated contacts: ______________________________

____

Observer's comments: ______________________________

____

Signature of observer: ______________________________

SPECIAL NOTE: *This form can be combined with a sociogram for a clear and very powerful record of the social interaction of a particular student within the classroom and may be very helpful in a student's evaluation.*

SCIENCE FAIR

Page One: Letter to Participants and Parents

Dear Future Scientist:

The West Falls Science Curriculum Committee and the West Falls P.T.A. are pleased to announce the dates for the West Falls School District's Annual Science Fair. The Fair will be held on Wednesday, May 9 and Thursday, May 10, 19XX at the West Falls Elementary School All-Purpose Room from 3:00 to 5:00 P.M. and then from 7:00 to 9:00 P.M.

This year it is required that all students from grades 4–8 submit a project. The students from grades K–3 may submit a project if they wish.

Both committees have recommended that parents, family, and teachers only give advice in the development of the project.

Your science teacher, homeroom teacher, and I will be happy to answer any questions you may have.

Good luck with your project...and see you at the Fair!

Sincerely,

SPECIAL NOTE: This page and the five that follow make an ideal package to distribute to all Science Fair participants. As you will see on page two, there is a return from parents, which insures that everybody knows exactly what is going on.

Page Two: Statement of Philosophy with Return

PHILOSOPHY

Science provides and important way for a child to experience the world. Since the world of tomorrow will be vastly different from our world of today, we must help children to develop a scientific process of thinking and a flexibility that will involve the creative problem-solving process. There is no better area in the entire school curriculum than Science through which to foster these skills.

Our Science Fair is an opportunity for every child in the West Falls Schools system to have a positive experience in Science. Projects are to be the child's selection and work. They should reflect each child's individual interest in this field. All children can appreciate and participate in the field of Science.

On the following pages are the rules for the Science Fair. After reading and discussing these rules with your child, please sign and return the form below.

We have read the rules for the Science Fair.

________________________ ________________________

(Child's name) (Parent's name)

SPECIAL NOTE: It is always a good idea to tell everyone exactly why an activity such as this is worthwhile.

Page Three: Rules for Participants

RULES

1. Students in all grades may enter a project in any area of scientific study. Exhibits will be judged by grade levels.
2. Each entry, no matter how it is displayed, must be accompanied by a report, a paper, or an explanation of the project. (Naturally, we will expect a more detailed report from an eighth grader, as opposed to a simpler explanation from a first grader's project.)
3. Only one exhibit per student will be allowed. Group projects will be limited to two students per group.
4. Although a child can accept suggestions and ideas from his or her parents or family, the child should put the project together him- or herself.
5. Exhibits must be limited in size to 30 inches front to back and 48 inches side to side. Floor space can be made available upon request.
6. Construction must be durable; moving parts must be firmly attached and safe.
7. All switches and cords must be of an approved variety. All exhibits needing electricity must provide a six-foot extension cord with the standard style parallel plug.
8. Dangerous chemicals, open flames, explosive, and poisonous reptiles will not be allowed.
9. Animals must be fed and watered and cages must be cleaned daily. Plants must be watered daily.
10. Experiments on animals must conform with the "Regulations Governing Experiments on Animals," which is enclosed.
11. Scoring will be based on work done by exhibitors, *not on the value of accessory equipment either borrowed or purchased.*
12. Judges will evaluate the exhibits immediately following setup. Only the judges and the rules committee will be permitted in the exhibit area during judging. Judges' decisions will be final.
13. The Science Fair Committee, the P.T.A., the Science Department, members of the professional staff, the Administration, and the Board of Education will not be held responsible for lost or damaged equipment or displays.
14. Any exhibit found not complying with the rules and regulations governing the Science Fair will be removed from the area by the Science Fair Committee (and may be picked up at the principal's office).

Page Three: Rules for Participants (Continued)

15. Exhibitors' names shall not appear anywhere on the display or report. All exhibits will be identified by a number.
16. Any method of display is acceptable. For instance: machines, experiments, collections, clay models, papier-maché models, pictures, cutaways, cross sections, posters, dioramas, panoramic models of any type, soil displays, and charts.
17. At the end of the Science Fair, all students must pick up their exhibits and remove them from the area.

SPECIAL NOTE: *As you look over these rules, note that they are reasonable, easily complied with by both parents and students, and quickly understood. Naturally, you may want to include some special rules of your own.*

Page Four: Regulations Concerning Animals

REGULATIONS GOVERNING EXPERIMENTS WITH ANIMALS

1. The aim of experimenting with animals shall be to achieve an understanding of life and life processes, leading to a respect for life.
2. No experiments shall be undertaken that involve anesthetic drugs, surgical procedures, pathogenic organisms, toxicological products, or radiation.
3. The comfort of the animal used in any study shall be of prime concern. Gentle handling, proper feeding, and provision of sanitary quarters shall at all times be strictly observed.
4. Any experiment in nutritional deficiency may proceed only to the point where symptoms of deficiency appear. Appropriate measures shall then be taken to correct the deficiency.
5. All animals are to be fed and watered and their cages cleaned daily during the Science Fair.
6. Students will be responsible for the caring of their animals.

Teachers will not be permitted to lend any equipment to any student.

SPECIAL NOTE: There exists considerable concern over the use of animals in scientific experimentation. These rules seem to allow for the knowledge gained from science with an eye toward the humane treatment of animals.

Page Five: Judging Form for Grades K–6

JUDGE'S SHEET (K–6)

Exhibit Number	Scientific Knowledge 25 points	Neatness 15 points	Completion 15 points	Accuracy 15 points	Research 15 points	Originality 15 points	TOTAL

SPECIAL NOTE: The advantage of putting the judge's form in the package that students take home to their parents is that everyone will know exactly how much each phase of the experiment or project will be worth in the judging.

Page Six: Judging Form for Grades 7–8

JUDGE'S SHEET (7–8)

Exhibit Number	Scientific Knowledge 25 points	Depth of Research 25 points	Neatness 10 points	Completion 10 points	Accuracy 10 points	Originality 10 points	Dramatic Appeal 10 points	TOTAL

SPECIAL NOTE: Notice that the criteria changes slightly for the upper elementary grades, which is as it should be. We expect our upper elementary students to have learned a bit in both knowledge and self-discipline along the way.

STUDENT COUNCIL

Statement of Purpose

The Thornton Junior High School Student Council is organized on the basis of homeroom representatives headed by five students called the Executive Board and are advised by a faculty member. All students are given an equal chance to be homeroom representatives, and elections are held late in the year to elect Student Council Officers for the following school year. Any student can, at any time, submit ideas to the Student Council Executive Board.

Participation in Student Council activities provides each student with an opportunity to offer valuable service to the school and to develop those characteristics of leadership so vital to the American way of life.

SPECIAL NOTE: This would be the type of statement you might place in a club charter for the school or in a student handbook.

TEACHER'S AIDE

Request for Services

Teacher: ____________________ Date: __________

Room: ________ Grade or subject: ____________________

I hereby formally request that a teacher's aide be assigned to me.

Subject: ______________________________

____

Time (periods; time of day; etc.): ____________________

____

Day(s): ______________________________

Expected duties of teacher's aide: ____________________

____

Other: ______________________________

____

SPECIAL NOTE: If you must make a formal written request for a teacher's aide in your district, then use this form in one of two ways. Use it as is, or use it to write down all the pertinent information you would have to include in a formal letter of request.

VISION

Report to Nurse

Teacher: ______________________________ Date: ______________

Student: ______________________________ Grade: ______________

Age of student: ______________ Homeroom: ______________________

I have reason to believe that the student named above may have a vision problem.

I have observed the following: ______________________________
____
____

I hereby request that this student be vision tested and the results

( ) BE PROVIDED TO ME ONLY
( ) BE SENT TO PARENTS ONLY
( ) BE SENT TO ME AND THE PARENTS

SPECIAL NOTE: This form provides all the data the nurse or health officer should know as well as your input as to what you have directly observed. Quite often, children will be unaware that a problem exists or be reluctant to tell anyone, so it is your duty to be on the lookout for these problems.

YEARBOOK

Advisor's Message

A yearbook is more than printed pages, clever sayings, and photographs. It is, in a very real sense, a record of memories—your memories—the memories you hold both individually and in common as students of Rock Township High School. It is my sincere hope as well as the hope of every member of the yearbook staff that those memories are pleasant ones, ones that you will cherish throughout your life. It is our hope that your days here at Rock Township High School have been enjoyable as well as filled with learning and growth. You have received an education that will serve you well throughout your lives, and the memories within these pages will serve you in those quiet moments when you turn your thoughts and hearts back to your days spent within these halls.

May health, happiness, and success be yours throughout your lives.

Sincerely,

SPECIAL NOTE: Serving as a yearbook advisor is no easy task. This is an advisor's message that was used on the second page of the book, right after the title page. It set the tone for the body of the book to follow.